SMITHSONIAN BOOK OF

NATIONAL

WILDLIFE

REFUGES

ERIC JAY DOLIN

PHOTOGRAPHS BY JOHN AND KAREN HOLLINGSWORTH

SMITHSONIAN BOOK OF
NATIONAL
WILDLIFE
REFUGES

SMITHSONIAN INSTITUTION PRESS · Washington and London

COPY EDITOR: Betsy Hovey
PRODUCTION EDITOR: E. Anne Bolen
DESIGNER: Janice Wheeler

Library of Congress Cataloging-in-Publication Data
Dolin, Eric Jay.
Smithsonian book of national wildlife refuges / Eric Jay Dolin :
photographs by John and Karen Hollingsworth.
p. cm.
Includes bibliographical references (p.)
ISBN 1-58834-117-8
1. Wildlife refuges—United States. 2. National Wildlife Refuge System
(U.S.) I. Title: National Wildlife refuges.
II. Title.
QL84.2.D65 2003
333.95'16'0973—dc21   2002030254

British Library Cataloguing-in-Publication Data is available

Manufactured in the United States of America
10 09 08 07 06 05 04 03   5 4 3 2 1

∞ The paper used in this publication meets the minimum requirements
of the American National Standard for Information Sciences—
Permanence of Paper for Printed Library Materials ANSI Z39.48-1984.

Unless otherwise credited in individual captions, all photographs are the
property of John and Karen Hollingsworth. For permission to reproduce
illustrations appearing in this book, please correspond directly with the
owners of the works. The Smithsonian Institution Press does not retain
reproduction rights for these illustrations individually, or maintain a file
of addresses for photo sources.

HALF-TITLE PAGE: Glaucous-winged gull nest with eggs at the Protection Island NWR, Washington.

TITLE PAGE: An autumn evening with waterfowl and white-tailed deer at the Kirwin NWR, Kansas.

LEFT: Canada geese among fall cypress at the Cypress Creek NWR, Illinois. This refuge lays claim to the oldest living stand of trees east of the Mississippi, which includes cypress trees that have been around for more than a millennium.

DEDICATION PAGE: Kodiak brown bear feasting on salmon at the Kodiak NWR, Alaska.

CONTENTS: Migrating monarch butterflies feeding on milkweed at the Edwin B. Forsythe NWR, New Jersey.

TO MY PARENTS,
STANLEY AND RUTH DOLIN,
WHO ALWAYS TAUGHT ME
TO ASK QUESTIONS.

—EJD

TO THE DIRT AND THOSE
WHO WORK TO SAVE IT.

—KH

CONTENTS

ACKNOWLEDGMENTS

Every book is built upon the shoulders of others. This book benefited immensely from the work of numerous authors and even more individuals who shared their knowledge of and love for the National Wildlife Refuge System. The authors are given their due in the bibliography, and to them we offer a sincere thank you. Among those individuals who provided support and information, six deserve special thanks. Dan Ashe, chief of the National Wildlife Refuge System, and James Kurth, deputy chief of the National Wildlife Refuge System, believed in this project, helped to get it off the ground, and worked with us to make sure we had access to the resources we needed. Bill Reffalt, former head of the Refuge Division and serious student of the history of the refuge system, not only provided extensive background information but also commented on early drafts of the manuscript and offered encouragement and advice throughout the project. Kevin Kilcullen, historic preservation officer, was a key contact at the U.S. Fish and Wildlife Service, and he helped us gather information and locate

Red fox pups at the Agassiz NWR, Minnesota.

sources within and outside the service. Anne Post Roy, librarian at the service's National Conservation Training Center, was kind enough to let Eric borrow numerous books and articles from the center's library, a courtesy that made researching and writing the book much easier. And Jim Clark, editor of the *Refuge Reporter,* graciously provided copies of his excellent publication as source materials.

Other individuals within the Fish and Wildlife Service who were critical to the success of this book include James Bell, Terry Bell, Bill Buchanan, Jacqueline Burns, Jeff Drahota, Pauline Drobney, Marilyn Gamette, George Garris, Nancy Gilbertson, Layne L. Hamilton, Mike Hedrick, Elizabeth Jackson, Joyce Kleen, Margaret T. Kolar, James G. Kraus, Carmen Leong, Rachel Levin, Mark Madison, Randy Matchett, Barbara A. Maxfield, Carl Mitchell, Lauri S. Munroe, Anita Noguera, Maggie O'Connell, Daniel Perry, Dennis E. Prichard, Jennifer Rabuck, Skippy Reeves, John Schroer, Jerry Serie, Sandy Spakoff, Janet Tennyson, Angela V. Tracy, Lavonda Walton, Larry Wargowsky, and Joe Witt.

Many people outside of the refuge system provided invaluable assistance. They include the following: Kip Koss, grandson of J. N. "Ding" Darling, who graciously allowed us to reproduce some of his grandfather's cartoons; George Laycock, freelance writer and chronicler of the refuge system; Heather Ray, Joseph Duff, and Deke Clark from Operation Migration; Wallace Finley Daily, curator of the Theodore Roosevelt Collection at the Houghton Library of the Harvard College Library; Robert M. Chipley from the American Bird Conservancy; Mary Seldon from the Wilderness Society; Dawn Eurich from the Detroit Public Library; Doris Gove, nature writer; Meagan Shaw from the Chesapeake Bay Maritime Museum; Keri Langille and Kim Smith from the C. M. Russell Museum; Evan Hirsche and Gretchen Muller from the National Wildlife Refuge Association; and Frank Herch, George Franchois, and Jennifer Klang, librarians at the U.S. Department of the Interior Library.

Bob Dumaine, Eric's coauthor for *The Duck Stamp Story: Art-Conservation-History* (Krause Publications, 2000), also deserves sincere thanks. If it weren't for Eric having worked on that book, which exposed him to the wonders of the refuge system, he never would have come up with the idea of doing this book. Another special thanks goes to Marty Christian, former senior editor at the National Geographic Society Book Division, who was one of the first people to say this book was a great idea. Her encouragement and advice helped us keep pitching the book until we hooked a publisher.

Vincent Burke, our editor at the Smithsonian Institution Press, was a great supporter of the book and offered gentle assistance throughout the project, for which we are most grateful. Assistant Editor Nicole Sloan also has our gratitude. Copy Editor Betsy Hovey, Production Editor Anne Bolen, and Design Manager Janice Wheeler provided suggestions, insights, and design skills that greatly improved the book. And to the five anonymous reviewers, thank you for your excellent comments.

For Eric the most important support for this project came from his wife, Jennifer, and children, Lily and Harry. Eric could not have written this book if his family had not made it possible for him to carve out time early in the morning, late at night, and on the weekends to write. Jennifer served as a sounding board for ideas, reviewed drafts, offered encouragement and humor, and never complained. Although Lily (five) and Harry (three) didn't have much advice on the content of the book, they did often spur on their dad. Many times, one or both of them said, "daddy go downstairs and work," and then visited him later in his basement office to see

how things were going. Without the love and support of his family, Eric's dream of writing this book would have remained just that.

For Karen the idea of creating an image-rich book celebrating the centennial of the refuge system began many years ago as she and John became more and more immersed in refuges. The wildlife and wildlands captivated them as nature photographers, but the dedicated Fish and Wildlife Service employees managing these remarkable lands and the grassroots cadre of citizens volunteering their time and talents are the glue that kept them "stuck." The people of the refuge system have become family, and without their interest, guidance, encouragement, trust, time, moral support, and lasting friendships forged over the past eighteen years, recording these "moments in time" on film would have been impossible. Karen can't begin to mention everyone by name because it would take up the entire book, but her respect and gratitude run deep.

Karen also acknowledges two remarkable men in her life, John Hollingsworth and Doug Grann. Over many years she and John honed their photographic talents side by side, encouraging and critiquing, traveling thousands of miles together and separately, each one's style and vision different yet complementing the other's, creating a body of work that by the time of John's untimely death was unsurpassed in its coverage of the refuge system. This book reflects the depth of that perseverance. In choosing to continue her work on refuges, Karen is now blessed with the love and support of her husband, Doug Grann, who shares her passion for the wild and always welcomes the opportunity for yet another adventure.

Finally, in addition to those listed above, we would like to thank all of the people who have supported and worked on behalf of the refuge system through the years. It is our hope that this book will add to their ranks.

A pair of common loons at the Lake Umbagog NWR, New Hampshire.

A NATIONAL TREASURE

It is hereby ordered that Pelican Island in Indian River in section nine, township thirty-one south, range thirty-nine east, State of Florida, be, and it is hereby reserved and set apart for the use of the Department of Agriculture as a preserve and breeding ground for native birds.

President Theodore Roosevelt, March 14, 1903

This simple, unremarkable declaration, a mere forty-eight words, although heartily welcomed by many, was not a major event at the time. The press did not trumpet the news. There was no sense that this was the beginning of something that would produce immeasurable benefits for generations to come. Yet by affixing his signature, Roosevelt officially launched the National Wildlife Refuge System, which is the only network of federal lands dedicated to wildlife conservation. The refuge system is truly an American original. There is nothing else like it in the world.

Great blue heron at sunset at the Ottawa NWR, Ohio.

Draped over the land like a vast strand of glittering jewels, the refuge system is one of the greatest of America's natural treasures. Its 538 refuges

and thousands of waterfowl production areas contain 95 million acres, an area larger than the National Park System and about the same size as the state of Montana. There are refuges in every state and many U.S. territories and possessions, and they range in size from the diminutive 0.6-acre Mille Lacs National Wildlife Refuge (NWR) in Minnesota to the enormous Arctic NWR that extends over 19.6 million acres of the Alaskan landscape. The refuge system offers an impressive array of habitats—barrier islands, bogs, caves, coastal lagoons, coral reefs, deserts, estuaries, hardwood forests, islands, lakes, meadows, mountains, ponds, rocky coastlines, salt marshes, sand dunes, swamps, tallgrass prairies, and tundra. These habitats protect, nourish, replenish, and restore thousands of species of birds, mammals, reptiles, amphibians, fish, and plants, many of which are endangered and hanging on to survival by the weakest of threads.

The refuge system is a priceless gift. It reflects the great diversity of the tapestry of life and the commitment of the United States to wildlife conservation. Wherever visitors go in the refuge system, they will experience a sense of wonder and the joy that comes from nature's company. Each refuge has the power to fill up their senses and stir their souls through sights and sounds beautiful and sublime. At Oklahoma's Wichita Mountains Wildlife Refuge, the earth trembles as a herd of buffalo thunders past. In the deep blue waters of the Crystal River NWR in Florida, a manatee glides slowly over the ocean's floor in search of plants to eat. The wild ponies graze near the shoreline at the Chincoteague NWR in Virginia. And at the Hatchie NWR in Tennessee there are scarlet tanagers, yellow warblers, ruby-crowned kinglets, indigo buntings, goldfinches, and green-backed herons and an orchestra's worth of songbird serenades.

The beauty and diversity of the refuge system

Lupines and Red Rock Pass at the Red Rock Lakes NWR, Montana. This refuge is usually snowed in from Thanksgiving through mid-April, under accumulations of up to 150 inches of snow.

Shelf fungus at the Ace Basin NWR, South Carolina.

RIGHT: The endangered prairie white-fringed orchid blooms at the Valentine NWR, Nebraska.

come through in the names of refuges. Those honoring Native American Indians have a lyrical cadence and mystical quality that evoke some of the saddest passages in this country's history— Mattamuskeet, Mashpee, Havasu, Iroquois, and Shiawassee. There are refuges named after famous Americans whose lives have enriched everyone's—John James Audubon, Rachel Carson, Senator John H. Chafee, and Lewis and Clark. Other refuges are labeled more prosaically, highlighting geographic locations or particular species—Gray's Harbor, Cape Romain, Three Arch Rocks, Oregon Islands, Attwater Prairie Chicken, Ozark Cavefish, Florida Panther, and the National Bison Range.

The history of the refuge system, which is administered by the U.S. Department of the Interior's Fish and Wildlife Service, mirrors this country's fascinating, colorful, dramatic, at times disastrous, and often inspirational relationship with wildlife. The refuge system has grown more opportunistically than strategically. Decade after decade, a combination of executive orders, statutes, direct purchases, and donations have added refuges and acreage to the refuge system. All the while, this amazing network of lands has been buffeted by conflicting imperatives, budgetary and natural droughts, management problems, organizational changes, and the mounting pressures of protecting itself from the increasingly potent threats posed by population growth and development.

The refuge system has succeeded, first and foremost, because of the amazing and too often unheralded dedication and hard work of its employees, those whom the American people have, in effect, hired to be caretakers of a significant part of the country's wildlife heritage. The refuge system is also indebted to untold thousands of other government employees, politicians, nonprofit organizations, and volunteers who not only believed in it but also fought to make it work by turning obstacles into opportunities. The fruits of their labors are on view every day.

The numbers of migratory waterfowl that rest, feed, and breed on refuges have swelled to all-time highs from all-time lows. Large game such as bison, elk, and pronghorn antelope are prospering on refuges in the American West. Tens of millions of acres in the refuge system are designated as wilderness, places where human impact is minimal and nature approaches its original state. Through active management, marginal refuge lands have been transformed into productive areas that benefit all the species that live in or migrate through them. Scores of refuges are providing habitat necessary for endangered species to survive and thrive. And on virtually every refuge in the country, any time of year, the magnificent rhythms of nature are played out with heartening regularity: a mouse digging a burrow, a jellyfish undulating through sun-flecked water, a swan alighting on a still lake, a mother bear protectively watching over its cubs, and a mighty tree swaying in the breeze before a coming storm. Simple events, perhaps, but ones as important as the greatest works of humanity.

Although wildlife comes first on refuges, they are also the people's lands, intended for the recreation and enjoyment of all. Visitors may see binoculars raised in unison as a group of patient birders spies a rare species on a distant branch. A boy and his father casting into the deep waters of a cold lake creating memories and hoping for a fish to bite. Hikers in a wilderness area standing on the spine of an exposed ridge and seeing nothing but the natural landscape in every direction. Schoolchildren listening in rapt attention as a refuge volunteer talks about the species they are likely to see on their nature walk. A photographer zooming in on a hillside and with a quick press of a button capturing forever the image of a bighorn sheep bounding across rough terrain. And, on the edge of a marsh, two hunters waiting silently in a blind for geese to arrive.

Every year nearly forty million people visit refuges for a special experience. But humanity's interactions with the refuge system are often less personal. Oil and gas drilling, mining, farming, grazing, timbering, and military exercises are also acceptable activities on refuge lands as long as they don't interfere with the purposes for which the refuge was established. The varied use of refuges is a strength as well as a weakness. The refuge system provides numerous benefits but is often stressed and strained in doing so. This is part of the dynamic tension that makes managing the refuge system such a challenging task.

Strangely, for lands that have provided so many benefits for so long, the refuge system is relatively unknown to many Americans. It is largely a hidden treasure, but it shouldn't be. The refuge system is arguably the best way to ensure that current and future generations have an opportunity to appreciate the glory of wild America. This archipelago of diverse habitats is an integral part of this country's intimate connection to wildlife and wild places. It helps to define the character and values of the United States, and it deserves respect, support, and admiration.

2

FROM ABUNDANCE TO SCARCITY

Whereas the creation of the Pelican Island Reservation on March 14, 1903, officially launched the National Wildlife Refuge System, the latter's true origins reach back to the colonial era and then follow the tendrils of history through the early 1900s. In that relatively short span of time, a mere blip in the history of the land, the colonists and their descendants transformed the New World and subdued nature to an astonishing degree. Wildlife once thought to be inexhaustible was pushed up to and sometimes over the brink of extinction. The notion of protecting and preserving wildlife from the ravages of civilization moved from the realm of isolated necessity to the point of being a widely accepted idea whose time had come.

The abundance of wildlife, especially in comparison with the denuded forests and picked over lands of the Old World, amazed the first European settlers on the eastern shores of what was to become the United States. In 1607 colonist John Percy looked skyward near Jamestown, Virginia, and observed an "abundance of Fowles of all kindes, they flew over our heads as thicke as drops of hale; besides they made such a noise, that wee

Annual bison roundup at the Fort Niobrara NWR, Nebraska.

White pelicans at the Tule Lake NWR, California.

RIGHT: A Currier and Ives print showing a hunter patiently waiting for a good shot. *Library of Congress.*

were not able to heare one another speake." Thomas Morton, who landed in Boston Harbor in 1624, called his surroundings "nature's Masterpeece" and concluded that "If this land not be rich, then is the whole world poore." The Reverend Francis Higginson in 1630 observed that "The abundance of Sea-Fish are almost beyond beleeving, and sure I should scarce have beleeved it except I had seene it with mine owne eyes." William Wood, writing in 1634 about the wonders of the "New England," stated, "If I should tell you how some have killed a hundred geese in a week, fifty ducks at a shot, forty teals at another, it may be counted impossible though nothing more certain." Of all the species that inspired awe, none surpassed the passenger

pigeon, whose annual migrations blanketed the sky. John Josselyn wrote in 1673, "I have seen a flight of pidgeons in the spring . . . for four or five miles that to my thinking had neither beginning nor ending, length or breadth, and so thick I could see no Sun."

Many early colonists were misleading about what they encountered in an effort to promote colonial endeavors and lure others from their country to follow in their footsteps. To lower the expectations of potential immigrants, some colonists qualified the accounts they sent back to Europe. Writing in 1628, Christopher Levett stated, "I will not tell you . . . that the deer come when they are called, or stand still and look on a man until he shoot him, not knowing man from beast . . . [nor] that the fowls will present themselves to you with spits through them." Early colonists cannot be faulted for believing that wildlife could not be depleted no matter the actions of man. There was no sense of boundaries or limits, and from a practical point of view, there were none. The landscape stretched out farther than the eye could see, and beyond every mountain and valley, and through every glade and forest, the natural wealth of the land poured forth in glorious profusion. The steady erosion of this wealth, however, began immediately.

Pressures on wildlife came from many quarters. The colonists needed meat, and wildlife provided it. They required land for crops and buildings and roads, and every acre that was tilled or consigned to progress was one less acre of natural habitat. Colonial hunters turned the sights of their guns on wild game to fill their pots and satisfy their desire for sport. In 1621 Edward Winslow of the Massachusetts Colony advised new immigrants and sportsmen to come

prepared for excellent waterfowling near Plymouth. "Let your piece [musket] be long in the barrel and fear not the weight of it, for most of our shooting is done from stands." The market hunters, who shot for profit, busily plied their trade, and business was good. Morton, one of the first market hunters, said that he often "had one thousand Geese before the muzzle of . . . [his] gun." Goose and swan feathers for quilting and featherbeds were in great demand in Europe, and the growing population in the colonies generated a strong demand for fresh meat, which the market hunters gladly supplied.

From the mid-1600s through the 1700s, the colonists spread north and south and west toward the shifting frontier in ever-increasing numbers. The pressures on wildlife continued and changed more in degree than kind. Larger populations meant more building, more cropland, and more mouths to feed. Market hunters kept pace with the rising demand for their services here and abroad. The ranks of subsistence

Dr. Harry Walsh holding two punt guns. These enormous guns could kill scores of birds with a single shot.

RIGHT: Skiff equipped with battery gun and gunning light.

BELOW: Postcard printed around the turn of the nineteenth century showing Jesse Poplar in action in a sink box on Chesapeake Bay, near Havre de Grace, Maryland. He was one of the best-known wing shots and market hunters of the day. An article appearing in the November 1, 1893, edition of the *Baltimore Sun* recounts one of his outings when he killed five thousand ducks in a single day, taking most of the birds from a sink box. He and his partner, who manned the pickup boat, split $150 for their efforts, a considerable sum at that time. While sink boxes were effective for hunting, they were susceptible to swamping in rough weather. An errant discharge of a hunter's gun could quickly send the boat to the bottom and seriously injure the hunter.

Harry Walsh Collection, Chesapeake Bay Maritime Museum.

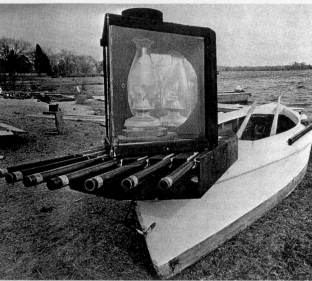

hunters in search of food to feed their families also increased, and both of these groups operated largely unfettered by legal restrictions on the amount of game that could be taken.

During this period only a hint of the coming devastation was apparent. A handful of jurisdictions saw fit to restrict hunting to protect certain animals. For example, in 1705 the General Assembly of Rhode Island expressed its concern about the illegal taking of deer. "It hath been informed that great quantities of deer hath been destroyed in this Collony out of season . . . and may prove too much to the damage of this Collony for the future, and . . . for the whole

country, if not prevented." In 1708 a few counties in central New York instituted the first closed season on birds, protecting the heath hen, ruffed grouse, turkey, and quail. Two years later, Massachusetts prohibited the use of camouflaged canoes or sailboats in the pursuit of waterfowl. In 1772, Virginia, fearing that deer hunting was exterminating local populations, suspended deer hunting for four years to allow the animals to recuperate. And, in 1797, Vermont enacted a law protecting muskrats, much in demand for their pelts, from hunting during the months of June, July, and August. But such laws were few in number and of questionable impact due to a frequent lack of enforcement.

In the 1800s the balance between human progress and the survival of wildlife shifted decidedly against wildlife. The myth of the inexhaustible supply of birds and animals was shot down figuratively and literally. The basic storyline was familiar. Pressures on wildlife came from the increase in market hunting and, to a lesser extent, sport hunting, as well as the destruction of habitat through the dramatic expansion of cities, towns, farms, and roads. In the war between human needs and desires and nature and its limits, wildlife was being routed.

The advent of the railroad in the early nineteenth century spurred the march of humanity across the landscape and further closed the loop between the suppliers of wildlife products and their markets. The railroad also transported hunters closer to their game. Not only were hunters going farther and faster than ever before in their pursuit of wildlife but they were doing so with more efficient and deadlier tools. Around 1820, muzzle-loading caplock guns began replacing the less reliable and accurate flintlock rifles. Other larger and more deadly guns also came into use at this time. The most horrific was the cannonlike punt gun that could

throw a pound of shot per firing, killing upwards of one hundred birds. Just as deadly was the so-called battery, an array of gun barrels mounted on the bows of small watercraft. In the hands of eager market hunters, punt guns and batteries

Shooting star at National Bison Range, Montana.

could devastate entire flocks of ducks and geese. In the 1870s faster-action and more accurate breech-loading guns replaced the muzzleloaders, and by the century's end the common use of repeating shotguns made the killing of animals more efficient still.

The introduction of refrigerated train cars in the late 1800s added a whole new dimension to the plight of wildlife by greatly expanding the range over which market hunters could operate and still turn a profit. It also enabled the palates of consumers in one region of the country to become accustomed to the taste of game from other regions, thereby increasing demand for

wildlife and expanding the content of menus far and wide. At luxurious accommodations a truly astounding range of wildlife could be found on one's plate. On Thanksgiving 1886 John B. Drake, a Chicago hotel proprietor, offered his patrons a sumptuous game dinner that included a veritable who's who of animals. The "Procession of Game" ran from venison soup, leg of mountain sheep, ham of bear, buffalo tongue, blue-winged teal, leg of elk, and sandhill crane to antelope steak in mushroom sauce, oyster pie, fillet of grouse with truffles, and rabbit braise with cream sauce. As if that was not enough, the diners were surrounded by a variety of "ornamental dishes" that included a "Pyramid of Game en Bellvue, The Coon out at Night, and Boned Quail in Plumage."

The history of this so-called Age of Extermination is full of stories in which species of wildlife were eliminated from vast expanses of their historical ranges, killed in enormous numbers, or completely annihilated. By the 1840s the beaver, pursued relentlessly for its luxuriant pelt, was virtually extinct east of the Rocky Mountains. Great auks, large flightless birds that had summered in the millions along the northeastern coast of the United States, were mercilessly killed for their feathers, oil, and flesh by hunters, skin collectors, and fishermen who cut up the birds for cod bait. Unable to outrun their pursuers, the auks were easily dispatched with a swing of a club to the head. In early June 1844 the last two birds of this species ever seen were killed on a volcanic outcropping near the coast of Iceland, their skins sold to a Danish collector for £9. Elk and wild turkey, once plentiful in New York, had by the mid-1800s disappeared due to hunting pressures. At the time it was not unusual for gunners on the Chesapeake Bay to kill upwards of fifteen thousand ducks in a single day. Even the growing scarcity of game birds toward the end of the nineteenth century was not enough to stop the slaughter. As the supply of birds sank, the demand rose, and the higher the price paid for a duck or a goose, the harder the hunter worked to get paid. The most dramatic and oft-told stories of wildlife destruction in America involve the passenger pigeon and the bison, commonly called the buffalo. Better examples of humankind's ability to decimate wildlife are hard to find.

It has been estimated that there were between three and five billion passenger pigeons when the Europeans first came to America. By the early 1800s, even though this species had already been subjected to well over one hundred years of intensive killing, sightings of enormous flocks of pigeons were still common. In 1813 John James Audubon, the great artist and naturalist, traveling in Kentucky, claimed to have seen a flight of more than one billion birds. Observing a large roost of passenger pigeons was an awesome sight. The din was ear-splitting as wings fluttered, birds cooed, and branches, and in some cases entire trees of considerable girth crashed to the ground under the weight of thousands of pigeons alighting upon every available inch of sylvan real estate. Audubon wrote about a flock arriving "with a noise that sounded like a gale passing through the rigging of a close-reefed vessel." The droppings of roosting pigeons were so numerous that it looked as if the ground was cloaked in snow.

Ironically, the massive numbers of passenger pigeons played a part in their undoing. So numerous were they that when flocks descended on crops, they could quickly strip them bare. In Plymouth in 1643, pigeons consumed so much corn and grain that the area was pushed to the edge of famine. Farmers, viewing the feathered locusts as competition and thieves, killed as many as they could to maintain their livelihood. Passenger pigeons also had the misfortune, like so many imperiled species, of being easy to kill and tasty, a combination that made them a favorite item at stores and markets throughout the land. And, with such a great supply, passenger pigeons were cheap. In 1736 six could be had for a penny on the streets of Boston.

One particularly disturbing image of the pursuit of passenger pigeons in the late 1700s is offered in James Fenimore Cooper's book *The Pioneers,* set in 1793. Although the book is fictional, the scene is rooted in reality.

The reports of the firearms became rapid, whole volleys rising from the plain, as flocks of more

LEFT: John James Audubon is most famous for his drawings of birds and wildlife. These Canada geese and wood ducks are two of his most beautiful renditions of migratory waterfowl. *Library of Congress.*

John James Audubon.

than ordinary numbers [of passenger pigeons] darted over the opening [of a highway], shadowing the field like a cloud; and then the light smoke of a single piece would issue from among the leafless bushes on the mountain, as death was hurled on the retreat of affrighted birds, who were rising from a volley, in a vain effort to escape. Arrows, and missils of every kind, were in the midst of the flocks; and so numerous were the birds, and so low did they take their flight, that even long poles, in the hands of those on the sides of the mountain, were used to strike them to the earth. . . . None pretended to collect the game, which lay scattered over the fields in such profusion as to cover the very ground with the fluttering victims.

By the early 1800s the eastern flocks of pigeons were greatly diminished, but the flocks farther west remained strong, and the killing continued apace. While sportsmen or individuals looking for sustenance often used guns or poles to hunt pigeons, the professional market hunter almost always used baited nets that could capture hundreds of birds at once. Sometimes they would use live decoys perched on stools, which not only

drew the duped birds into the nets but also added the term *stool pigeon* to the American lexicon.

Efforts to stem the killing of the passenger pigeon were rare. When authorities considered the passenger pigeon at all, the need to protect the birds was not their concern. In 1848 the Massachusetts's legislature passed a law protecting pigeon *netters* by levying a fine on those impudent souls who frightened pigeons from nets. When in 1857 a legislator in Ohio offered a bill to restrict the killing of passenger pigeons, it was defeated. The committee report on the demise of the bill was brimming with confidence and certitude. "The passenger pigeon needs no protection. Wonderfully prolific, having the vast forests of the North as its breeding grounds, traveling hundreds of miles in search of food, it is here to-day and elsewhere to-morrow, and no ordinary destruction can lessen them or be missed from the myriads that are yearly produced." For a short time longer, it seemed as if this pronouncement was correct. In 1871 observers in Wisconsin witnessed the largest nesting of passenger pigeons ever documented, estimated as being 75 miles long and from 5 to 10 miles wide. And the birds could still be purchased for between $.15 and $.25 per dozen. The idea that the passenger pigeon might be in danger of extinction would have likely been viewed by contemporaries of the great Wisconsin nesting as absurd. For a few years more, passenger pigeons continued to congregate in enormous concentrations, and wherever they were found, hordes of market hunters were soon to follow. The number of birds killed was truly astounding. In 1875 netters from two Michigan counties sent 2,400,000 mature pigeons to market. In the same year a group of Ohio netters shipped between 40 and 50 tons of pigeons.

Those who thought this massive slaughter could continue indefinitely were in for a rude surprise. The last great gathering of passenger pigeons ever recorded took place in 1878. The birds landed near Petoskey, Michigan, and within a few weeks, 2,500 netters were able to kill and sell 1,107,800,066 pigeons. Never again would the pigeons be seen in such profusion. Never again would the market be deluged with the meat from these magnificent birds. Three years later, when netters descended upon another congregation of pigeons in Michigan, they could only kill a million, not because the netters' skills had diminished but because the number of birds had greatly decreased. During the next few decades, occasional flocks would be spotted, but they were mere fragments of the past—the last gasp of a dying species.

As late as May 1907, then-President Theodore Roosevelt reported looking skyward and seeing a dozen birds flying overhead near Pine Knot, his rustic vacation home close to Rapidan, Virginia. A less-trained eye might not have given them a second thought or mistakenly labeled them doves. But Roosevelt knew his birds and had no doubt. Their coloration, close flying formation, and silhouettes against the sky all identified them as passenger pigeons, a specimen of which he had studied in his youth. In that same afternoon Roosevelt saw the pigeons twice more, and then they were gone. Not too long after, the entire species was gone. In 1914 Martha, the last passenger pigeon, died at the age of twenty-nine at the Cincinnati Zoological Garden. Shortly before Martha's demise, in a last-ditch effort to save the species, a $1,000 reward had reportedly been offered to anyone who would capture a male pigeon to be Martha's mate, but it went unclaimed. The most numerous bird ever to exist, what famed twentieth-century wildlife biologist Aldo Leopold referred to as "a biological storm," was no more.

The bison nearly shared the passenger pigeon's fate. When the conquistadors were exploring the Great Plains, and even before the English had set foot on the eastern shores, there might have been up to one hundred million bison roaming the continent. Small offshoots of

COL.W.F.CODY

I AM COMING

Poster, circa 1900, announcing that William "Buffalo Bill" Cody and his Wild West Show were on the way. In an excerpt from one of his autobiographies, *Story of the Wild West and Camp-Fire Chats,* Cody recounts how he got his nickname:

> The construction of the end of the track got into the great buffalo country. . . . It was before the refrigerator car was in use and the contractor had no fresh meat to feed their employees. . . . I immediately began my career as a buffalo hunter for the Kansas Pacific Railroad, and it was not long before I acquired considerable notoriety. It was at this time that the very appropriate name of "Buffalo Bill" was conferred upon me by the railhands. It has stuck to me ever since, and I have never been ashamed of it.

Library of Congress.

the great western herds extended east as far as Virginia and Maryland. By the mid-1800s their numbers were already dwindling due to the great westward migration and the attendant increase in hunting. In 1843 Audubon made a prescient observation after watching a bison hunt on the western plains. "This cannot last. Even now there is a perceptible difference in the size of the herds. Before many years," he wrote, "the buffalo, like the Great Auk, will have disappeared; surely this should not be permitted."

The most intense assault on the bison commenced after the end of the Civil War. It came from many quarters: The army killed bison to starve out the Plains Indians; market hunters wanted the meat, hides, and tongues of the mighty beasts; cattlemen killed bison to keep

them from competing with their livestock for forage; the railroads hired men to kill them to supply meat for their workers and to fill up their freight cars with product; sportsmen killed for pleasure and to add a new trophy to the wall; and the Plains Indians, now mounted and using guns, killed bison more effectively than ever.

As with passenger pigeons the scope of the slaughter was almost unimaginable. Nearly one million bison were estimated to be killed in 1865. In 1871 and 1872 the annual kill was estimated to have risen to five million head. Buffalo Bill Cody, the most famous of the bison hunters, offered the following account of his efforts in the late 1860s to provide fresh meat to the Union Pacific Railroad.

> I had a wagon with four mules, one driver and two butchers, all brave, well-armed men, myself riding

This poster is circa 1899. Cody decided to launch his Wild West Show after achieving fame and fortune as the star of a traveling play about his life on the frontier that was based on the dime-store novels of Ned Buntline. According to Cody,

> Immense success and comparative wealth, attained in the profession of showman, stimulated me to greater exertion and largely increased my ambition for public favor. Accordingly, I conceived the idea of organizing a large company of Indians, cowboys, Mexican vaqueros, famous riders and expert lasso throwers, with accessories of stage coach, emigrant wagons, bucking horses, and a herd of buffaloes, with which to give a realistic entertainment of wild life on the plains.

Buffalo Bill's Wild West Show toured around the country and Europe to enthusiastic audiences. Cody died in 1917. *Library of Congress.*

my horse "Brigham." . . . I had to keep a close and careful lookout for Indians before making my run into a herd of buffalo. It was my custom in those days to pick out a herd that seemed to have the fattest cows and young heifers. I would then rush my horse into them, picking out the fattest cows and shooting them down . . . I killed buffalo for the railroad company for twelve months, and during that time the number I brought into camp was kept account of, and at the end of that period I had killed 4,280 buffalo.

The exploits of Cody and other bison hunters were romanticized in the press, but there was nothing romantic about them. Killing bison was usually mean, dirty work. And the way many of the bison were killed was incredibly wasteful. Untold numbers were simply shot from the windows of hunting cars on trains by tourists and "sportsmen" and left to rot. Whereas many bison were killed for their meat, others were killed only for their hides. After all, transporting hides was easier and just as, if not more, profitable than transporting butchered carcasses. But for some hunters the effort and time required to cut off and stake out a hide were too much, especially when there were so many bison and much easier money

to be made. With a knife, a hunter could extract a bison's tongue, a delicacy for which restaurant and hotel proprietors were willing to pay top dollar. The tongue was an even more appealing target because it was easily prepared in the field by smoking or salting and could be shipped by the barrel, taking up precious little of a train's cargo space.

So plentiful were the bleached skeletons of bison that they spawned secondary industries. Eager homesteaders earned income gathering skeletons and selling them to be sent to carbon companies where the bones were ground up into fertilizer

or used in the production of refined sugar. In Dodge City, where at one time it was estimated that two-thirds of its residents were involved in the bison hide trade, the mighty animal's bones were a legitimate form of money. Over a three-year period, from 1872 to 1874, the Atchison, Topeka, and Santa Fe Railroad alone transported 10,793,350 pounds of bison bones.

Despite this onslaught the number of bison roaming the plains was still impressive, although much reduced from earlier times. Colonel R. I. Dodge wrote that in the early 1870s he saw a herd "from the top of Pawnee Rocks" that spread out "from six to ten miles in almost every direction. This whole vast space was covered with buffalo, looking at a distance like a compact mass." Yet, like the passenger pigeon, the bison's final descent was swift.

In fall 1883, while on a hunting trip in the Bad Lands of the Dakota Territory, it took Theodore Roosevelt two weeks of trying before he shot his first bison, and prior to capturing that trophy, he and his guide hadn't even seen a bison—they were that scarce. Shortly thereafter, Roosevelt wrote,

> No sight is more common on the plains than that of a bleached buffalo skull; and their countless numbers attest the abundance of the animal at a time not so very long past. On those portions where the herds made their last stand, the carcasses, dried in the clear, high air, or the mouldering skeletons, abound. Last year, in crossing the country around the heads of the Big Sandy, O'Fallon Creek, Little Beaver, and Box Alder, these skeletons or dried carcasses were in sight from every hillock, often lying over the ground so thickly that several score could be seen at once. A ranchman who at the same time had made a journey of a thousand miles across northern Montana, along the Milk River, told me that, to use his own expression, during the whole distance he was never out of sight of a dead buffalo, and never in sight of a live one.

The decimation of the bison devastated the Native American population, spiritually and physically. Sadly, many welcomed this collateral

OPPOSITE, LEFT: Wood engraving depicting the practice of skinning bison. *Library of Congress.*

LEFT: An 1885 photo of Theodore Roosevelt in a deerskin hunting suit. *Library of Congress.*

ABOVE: A mountain of bison skulls near the train tracks in Detroit, Michigan, waiting to be hauled to the Michigan Carbon Works, circa the 1880s. *Courtesy of the Burton Historical Collection, Detroit Public Library.*

damage. For example, General Phil Sheridan, addressing the Texas legislature in 1875, lauded the impact that bison hunting was having on resolving the "Indian question." Hide hunters, he noted, had done more to beat back the Native Americans in two years than the army had done in thirty. "Let them kill, skin, and sell until the buffalo are exterminated. Then your prairies can be covered with speckled cattle and the festive cowboy, who follows the hunter as the second forerunner of an advanced civilization."

There were minor stabs at protecting the bison. In 1864 a closed season was instituted in western Idaho. In 1875 Kansas and Colorado prohibited hide hunting. A year earlier, Congress passed a bill to protect the bison, but President Ulysses S. Grant didn't sign it and it never came up again. It didn't matter. It was too late. At the end of the nineteenth century, the number of bison in the continental United States was in the low hundreds. In 1897, when the American Museum of Natural History realized it didn't have bison in the museum, it searched but couldn't find any, other than ones that were in private hands or part of the protected herd at Yellowstone National Park. The museum had to content itself with purchasing hides from cowboys and a taxidermist and accepting a single specimen from the National Museum and two others from Cody's Wild West show.

LEFT: Prairie pothole wetland in autumn at the Waubay NWR, South Dakota.

On May 3, 1933, an almost pure white buffalo calf was born on the National Bison Range. He was named Big Medicine in honor of the great sacred powers attributed to white bison by the Native Americans. Because Big Medicine had some pigmentation—tan hooves, brown topknot, and blue eyes—he was not a true albino. Nevertheless, his birth was an extremely rare event. Dr. William T. Hornaday said that he "had met many old buffalo hunters, who had killed thousands and seen scores of thousands of buffalo, yet had never seen a white one." The rarity of a white buffalo, perhaps a one in five million occurrence, made it all the more amazing that Big Medicine had been born to a herd that numbered only five hundred. Big Medicine lived until 1959, at which point he was sent to the taxidermist, was mounted, and is now on display at the Montana Historical Society Museum in Helena, Montana. *U.S. Fish and Wildlife Service.*

PRESERVATION, CONSERVATION, AND THE CALL TO ARMS

As the Age of Extermination wore on, public concern for wildlife and nature in general grew. In the mid-1800s transcendentalist philosophers, such as Henry David Thoreau and Ralph Waldo Emerson, extolled the virtues of living in harmony with the natural world. In a surprisingly prophetic article for the *Atlantic Monthly* in 1858, Thoreau offered thoughts on the establishment of "national preserves."

> The kings of England formerly had their forests "to hold the king's game," for sport or food . . . and I think that they were impelled by a true instinct. Why should not we, who have renounced the king's authority, have our national preserves . . . in which the bear and the panther, and some even of the hunter race, may still exist, and not be "civilized off the face of the earth"—our forests, not to hold the king's game merely, but to hold and preserve the king himself also, the lord of creation—not for idle sport or food, but for inspiration, and our own true recreation? Or shall we, like villains, grub them all up, poaching on our own national domains?

In the late 1800s John Muir gave eloquent voice to the preservationist movement, arguing that humankind's intrusion and impact on nature should be kept to a bare minimum. "How narrow we selfish, conceited creatures are in our

Snow geese by the thousands at the DeSoto NWR, Iowa.

23

Lillian Russell (*left*), 1861–1922, a famous singer and stage actor, and unidentified woman (*right*) wearing plumage on their hats. In 1897 a spirited series of letters on the use of bird feathers for adornment was published in the *New York Times*. On November 15 a person identified by the initials A. A. C. wrote,

> Is it possible that the women of New York are going to be the last in the country to give up wearing birds on their hats? . . . If only they stopped to think of the suffering they caused, I am sure they would be the first to give them up.

The next day A. B. C. responded.

> For some years I have been inclined to start an Anti-Audubon Society, and the contribution of . . . [A. A. C.] is one of several recent new incentives to carry out my intent. . . . Will any sensible being say why we women should not use any one of thousands of feathers and birds as adornment just as much as to wear furs of all animals?

Left: Library of Congress, photo by J. Schloss. Right: Denver Public Library, Western History Collection, RH-5902, photo by Harry M. Rhoads.

RIGHT: **Glaucous-winged gull nest with eggs at the Protection Island NWR, Washington.**

sympathies!" Muir wrote. "How blind to the rights of all the rest of creation!" Muir's love for wildlife, the land, and trees in particular spurred him to work tirelessly to protect nature's "cathedrals" and led him to launch the Sierra Club in 1892.

The increasingly desperate situation of wildlife toward the end of the nineteenth century spawned private efforts that would lead to the creation of the refuge system. This march toward the better protection of wildlife was headed by what on the surface appeared to be rather odd bedfellows—birdlovers and hunters. Although, for the most part, the two groups came at the problem from different perspectives, they worked toward many of the same goals and, in fact, had many members that claimed allegiance to both camps.

When the American Ornithologists Union (AOU) met for the first time on September 26, 1883, its membership was mainly concerned with tracking the distribution and migration patterns of birds, avian nomenclature and classification,

and investigating the economic importance of various species. But some of the AOU's members soon began agitating for the organization to work for the protection of birds that, in many cases, were being slaughtered at an alarming rate. To pursue this avenue, the AOU established the Committee on the Protection of North American Birds. The committee's efforts focused primarily on the feather trade, especially the use of bird plumes to adorn women's hats. In a bird committee bulletin from 1886, reprinted in *Science* magazine, a member of the committee ridiculed the practice of wearing bird parts that was all the rage.

> In this country of 50,000,000 inhabitants, half, or 25,000,000, may be said to belong to what some one has forcibly termed the "dead-bird wearing gender," of whom at least 10,000,000 are not only of the bird-wearing age, but—judging from what we see on our streets, in public assemblies and public conveyances—also of bird-wearing proclivities.

What they were seeing on the streets and other public places was an amazing array of avian finery, draped, hung, mounded, and otherwise

Great blue heron at the Blackwater NWR, Maryland.

impaled on the tops of women's hats. One observer, in only two strolls through a New York shopping district, counted 700 hats, of which 542 were festooned with birds of an amazing variety.

The bird committee was also appalled by the impact of "eggers" who collected eggs from shorebirds for the market trade or sustenance. In the same bulletin from 1886, another bird committee member sounded the alarm.

> Few persons living at a distance from the seashore have any idea of the immense destruction of bird-life by residents of the coast, who make the systematic and wholesale robbery of waterbirds of their eggs a yearly pastime. A thoughtless and relentless warfare has been waged, until the extermination of all bird-life on our shores stares us in the face.

The most amazing item in the bulletin was the presentation of the bird committee's Act for the Protection of Birds and Their Nests and Eggs, thereafter referred to as the Model Law. The committee had surveyed all the bird protection laws, which nearly every state had, and found them "crude and unsatisfactory so far as they relate to" nongame birds. The bird committee's problem with the laws had as much to do with their content as with their enforcement, or lack thereof.

> Defective as the present laws now generally are, they would, if thoroughly enforced, prevent the disgraceful slaughter now so general and untrammeled by any legal interference. . . . So apathetic is the public in all that relates to bird-protection, that prosecution under the bird-protection statutes requires, on the part of the prosecutor, a considerable amount of moral courage to face the frown of public opinion, the malignment of motive, and the enmities such prosecution is sure to engender.

The Model Law was intended to remedy the failures of existing laws by providing a template for states to adopt. Under the law a person who killed any nongame birds within the state, or who purchased, offered, or exposed for sale any such bird after it had been killed, would, for each offense, "be subject to a fine of five dollars, or imprisonment for ten days or both, at the discre-

tion of the court." Similar penalties were in store for anyone who took or needlessly destroyed the nest or eggs of any wild bird. Not surprisingly, given the fact that many AOU members were professional ornithologists who depended on eggs for study, the Model Law exempted from its strictures those who killed birds or collected eggs for certified scientific purposes.

This tiny Yakui chub at the San Bernardino NWR, Arizona, is one of the many species of endangered desert fishes protected on refuges.

RIGHT: Northern hardwood swamp at the Missisquoi NWR, Vermont.

The Model Law's focus on nongame birds was not an accidental oversight—it was intentional. The stated reason was because game birds, such as ducks and geese, were really birds of a different feather and they deserved to be subject to laws crafted and supported by sportsmen. Although this rationale could certainly stand on its own, there was another equally important reason for the omission. Many committee members were sport hunters as well as birdlovers, and they couldn't support a law that would ban their form of recreation. Even the nonhunters on the committee were well aware

that any law that banned game-bird hunting would be dead on arrival. Sportsmen were simply too powerful to be dismissed.

One of the most influential sportsmen on the committee was Dr. George Bird Grinnell. Born into wealth and raised in Audubon Park, New York, where Audubon, the artist and naturalist, spent his last days, Grinnell was educated about natural history by Audubon's widow, Lucy, and famed paleontologists at Yale University. He later became the publisher of the premier sporting publication in the country—*Forest and Stream*—and a man who had many friends in high places. Grinnell supported and quite likely helped to write the Model Law and, along with his colleagues at the AOU, pushed for its enactment nationwide. But Grinnell felt that the entreaties of the AOU and the implementation of protective legislation would not be enough to ensure the protection of the birds. He looked for inspiration to Dr. Joseph Asaph Allen, head curator at the American Museum of Natural History, who had argued that in order to halt the decline of many game and nongame species, societies should be set up throughout the country to work for the protection of such species. Grinnell also looked to England and saw how private individuals there had formed protective organizations that were having some success in getting the public and, therefore, the government more concerned about the plight of birds. Perhaps such activism could help turn the tide in the United States. To that end Grinnell wrote an editorial in *Forest and Stream,* published on February 11, 1886, in which he launched a new organization.

We propose the formation of an Association for the protection of wild birds and their eggs, which shall be called the Audubon Society. Its membership is to be free to everyone who is willing to lend a helping hand in forwarding the objects for which it is formed. These objects will be to prevent, so far as possible, (1) the killing of any wild birds not

used for food; (2) the destruction of nests or eggs of any wild birds; and (3) the wearing of feathers as ornaments or trimming for dress.

The Audubon Society soon claimed tens of thousands of members, all of whom received the society's high-quality *Audubon Magazine,* which was full of interesting articles and correspondences regarding birds and the need to protect them. One of the most famous essays, "Woman's Heartlessness," written by Celia Thaxter, was a scathing attack on the use of bird parts for women's apparel. After making a strong case for ending this sartorial practice, Thaxter ended

with a guarded optimism: "But still we venture to hope for a better future, still the Audubon and other societies work with heart and soul to protect and save them, and we trust yet to see the day when women, one and all, will look upon the wearing of birds in its proper light, namely, as a sign of heartlessness and mark of ignominy and reproach."

That day would come, but it was still far off in the future. After less than two years of fighting the good fight, Grinnell folded the Audubon Society. He and his *Forest and Stream* staff were overwhelmed by the added work required to publish the magazine and maintain correspondence with the expanding membership. The expense of maintaining the society was also a great drain. But Grinnell's decision was a reflection of weariness as well. Despite the attacks of Thaxter and her peers, the feather trade was flourishing. Grinnell gave voice to his frustrations in the final issue of the *Audubon Magazine:* "Fashion decrees feathers, and feathers it is. This condition of affairs must be something of a shock to the leaders of the Audubon Society, who were sanguine enough to believe that the moral idea represented by their movement would be efficacious to influence society at large."

The passions aroused by the Audubon Society did not end with the organization's dissolution. Grinnell had tapped a powerful vein of concern in American society. The AOU continued to argue against the feather trade and fight for the implementation of its Model Law. In 1896 the Massachusetts Audubon Society was formed. By the turn of the century, Audubon Societies had

sprung up in more than a quarter of the states. They too supported the Model Law and took up the cause against the feather merchants. And there were some successes. A number of states adopted the Model Law or strengthened existing laws. But on the eve of the twentieth century,

the focus of the fight for the protection of birds was already shifting away from the states to the federal government. The Audubon Societies, the AOU, and many others with allied interests believed that without federal intervention and support the cause of bird protection would fail. Many hunters, who were concerned not only about birds (especially migratory waterfowl) but also big game, joined them in this assessment.

In the late 1800s sportsmen went to great pains to distinguish themselves from the market hunters who killed game without restraint and for purely financial reasons. Although "true sportsmen" were honor bound by a sportsman's ethic as well as any laws that restricted hunting, the market hunter most certainly was not. Perhaps former president Grover Cleveland, an avid duck hunter, offered the best encapsulation of this view in 1906.

> There are those whose only claim to a place among duck hunters is based on the fact that they shoot ducks for the market. No duck is safe from their pursuit in any place, either by day or night. Not a particle of sportsmanlike spirit enters into this pursuit, and the idea never enters their minds that a duck has any rights that a hunter is bound to respect. The killing they do amounts to bald assassination—to murder for the sake of money. All fair-minded men must agree that duck hunters of this sort should be segregated from all others and placed in a section by themselves. They are the market shooters.

Sportsmen also disdained their peers who, while not market hunters, still killed with reckless abandon. As one observer at the turn of the century noted,

> unfortunately, there are men among the legion included under the title of sportsmen, as distinguished from market-gunners, who have never learned the virtue of moderation. They are never satisfied; they cannot kill enough. . . . The market-gunner has a poor business, but he has at least a tangible excuse for killing all he can. For the "game-hog" there is no extenuation, unless we credit him with a weak mind.

All that sportsmen of the day had to do was to

Muskrat feeding on bullrushes at the Modoc NWR, California.

RIGHT: Winter wetland sunrise at the Umatilla NWR, Oregon.

look around to see that their form of recreation, like many of the animals they hunted, was doomed to extinction unless measures were implemented to halt the slaughter. Here, again, Grinnell took a position of leadership. He used the pages of *Forest and Stream* to promote sportsmanlike behavior and rail against market hunters and game hogs. On February 3, 1894, he wrote,

> The game supply which makes possible the general indulgence in field sports is of incalculable advantage to individuals and the nation; but a game supply which makes possible the traffic in game as a luxury has no such importance. If this is granted, public policy demands that the traffic in game be abolished. . . . We suggest this declaration, the sale of game should be forbidden at all seasons, as a plank in the platform of that vast body of men scattered in hosts over the country . . . interested in preserving the game of the continent.

Forest and Stream was a powerful voice on the side of wildlife protection, and it forcefully advocated a range of measures. In addition to urging laws that would shut down the market hunters,

the newspaper also advocated the general enforcement of all wildlife protection laws and not just those pertaining to game animals. One issue that made repeated appearances in the pages of *Forest and Stream* throughout the 1890s was the need for federal game preserves where wildlife could multiply free from hunting. Such preserves would, in effect, serve as breeding grounds for depleted species and, in the process, replenish the populations upon which hunters depended for sport. The general call for preserves was wide-ranging, and it was heavily focused on the need to set aside preserves for game birds. In the June 5, 1897, issue of *Forest and Stream,* W. G. Van Name wrote,

> The state legislatures are clearly enough unable to make the laws necessary for the preservation of a [migratory] bird which breeds far to the north of our limits and passes twice a year through eight to ten states and several counties, venturing perhaps in Venezuela or Brazil. The idea naturally suggests itself that the taking of such birds and the protec-

tion of their eggs should be a subject for regulation by the National Government or even for International agreement. Though there is no probability of any such arrangement for a long time to come, yet it is very desirable that some effort should be made by the Government for their preservation.

Probably the most effective plan would be to have a series of reservations in different parts of the country where the birds would find a safe place to rest and feed during their stay here. Although this would not prevent the use of the land or water thus set apart for many purposes, it would be necessary to prohibit shooting entirely, at least during the season when the birds intended to be protected would be likely to be there. . . . There is not the least doubt that the birds would soon discover the greater security such reservations would offer, and would

show their appreciation of them by visiting them in increasing numbers and prolonging their stay.

In this amazingly foresighted article, Van Name rightly predicted that it would be some time, decades in fact, before effective national and international agreements were in place to protect migratory birds. His notion of setting aside preserves specifically for the protection of migratory game birds was also one that would simmer for decades. But when these ideas were put into action, they would have a dramatic impact on the growth and development of the refuge system.

Forest and Stream also called for the establish-

PROCEDING PAGES: Red-winged blackbirds in cattail marsh at dawn at the Merced NWR, California.

Wild roses blooming alongside a wetland at the Ruby Lake NWR, Nevada.

ment of marine reserves to protect endangered marine animals, including walruses, sea lions, seals, and salmon. President Benjamin Harrison gave the readers of the newspaper something to cheer about when on December 24, 1892, he signed a proclamation that set aside public land on Afognak Island in the Alaskan Territory to create a preserve to protect all the wildlife and plant life on and around the island, especially the salmon. The proclamation also stated that the preserve would be used to establish "fish culture stations" operated by the federal government. This was the second time the federal government had set aside land for the protection of wildlife. The first occurred on March 3, 1869, when Congress created a wildlife reservation in the Pribilof Islands in Alaska to protect fur seal rookeries. The protection afforded the seals, however, was not complete. In 1870, with Congress's blessing, the U.S. Treasury Department began leasing the rights to hunt the seals on the islands, a practice that led to decades of commercial operations in the area.

While *Forest and Stream* was trumpeting the concerns of sportsmen nationwide, another organization, the Boone and Crockett Club, had formed, the goals of which were similar to those of *Forest and Stream,* though narrower. The driving forces behind the formation of this new club were Theodore Roosevelt and Grinnell. In the mid-1880s Roosevelt, disconsolate after the deaths of his beloved wife, Alice, and his mother from illness on the same day, spent a great amount of time raising animals and hunting big game on his ranch in the Dakota Territory. In the fall of 1887, he embarked on a hunting trip and, in a replay of his earlier search for his first bison, came up nearly empty-handed. He encountered no grizzly or elk and precious few wild sheep. As a rancher he had seen, firsthand, how fences and grazing could destroy natural

habitat and cut the prairie into pieces. Also, as a hunter he had seen how hunting pressure from market hunters and greedy sportsmen could wipe out entire populations of big game. These two visions propelled Roosevelt to act. Upon his return to New York City later that year, he and Grinnell gathered together many of the nation's most eminent explorers, writers, scientists, and political leaders, all of whom shared a love of big-game hunting. This group became the base of the Boone and Crockett Club, launched at that meeting, which had the main goal of preserving big game in North America.

Club membership was set at one hundred and limited to men who, "in fair chase," had killed mature males of at least three species of big game in North America. Roosevelt and Grinnell and their equally famous fellow club members, including General William Tecumseh Sherman and painter Albert Bierstadt, used the art of gentle persuasion and lobbying to encourage politicians to pass laws protecting big game. One cause that the club threw its weight behind was the passage of the Yellowstone Park Protective Act. When the park was established in 1872, its main purpose was to preserve the scenic wonders of the region; there was no explicit legal protection afforded to the wildlife within its boundaries. It was realized early on that this was a problem, for the wildlife that is. Despite being protected by federal troops, Yellowstone National Park was still a favorite destination of poachers and market hunters in search of the hides and heads of bison and elk. The park, after all, had large elk herds and, after 1885, the only bison herd in the country of any significance. As early as 1883, legislation was introduced in Congress that would have made the park, in effect, an inviolate wildlife refuge. But it was not until 1894 that President Cleveland signed the Yellowstone Park Protective Act, which made the

park officially off-limits to any activities that would harm wildlife, and the killing of such wildlife was made an offense subject to jail sentences and fines.

The efforts of the AOU, the Audubon Societies, *Forest and Stream,* the Boone and Crockett Club, and other like-minded organizations and individuals combined to raise the cause of wildlife protection to that of a national crusade. By the end of the 1800s, one thread that tied all of these groups together was the firm belief that the states, on their own, did not have the will or power to stem the widespread slaughter of wildlife. The federal government, they argued, had to step in. At the turn of the century, the federal government finally did.

indeed, the federal government did do battle with those who sought to violate state laws, but it was facing a formidable foe. Money was still to be made in market hunting, and many men were more than willing to risk capture, especially when the risk was fairly low. Although the Lacey Act was impressive on paper, its effect in practice depended entirely on enforcement. Ironically, a law that had been passed because of lax enforcement suffered from an enforcement deficit itself. The Division of Biological Survey did its best, but there was only money for a relatively small number of game wardens, certainly not adequate to the task. Arrests were made, but they paled in comparison with the number of hunters who were not caught. Even if wardens were present on trains and at crossroads, there was no guarantee that violators would be found. Crafty market hunters would hide their birds in boxes labeled "eggs" or "butter" and further conceal the contraband with an actual layer of eggs or butter. Others transported illegally killed game in suitcases or trunks. But not all wardens were fooled. Some of them, well aware of the various ruses, would drill holes into boxes and luggage to confirm the nature of the contents, much to the dismay of the owners.

Of particular concern to the AOU and the state Audubon Societies, which had banded together in 1901 to form a loose federation called the National Committee of the Audubon Societies of America, was the failure of the Lacey Act to halt the use of feathers in the millinery trade. In the early 1900s one could still see, with astonishing regularity along the avenues and streets of cities both large and small, women's bonnets with birds on top. An ornithologist walking down Eighth Avenue in New York City noticed a woman wearing a hat with the following menagerie in tow: "Blackcock's tail, Dove's and Whip-poor-wills' wings,

Grebe's breast, Paradise Bird's plumes, a bunch of Aigrettes [the mating plume of a snowy egret], and a Hummingbird!" A Chicago reporter observing this fashion trend wrote, "it will be no surprise to me to see life-sized turkeys or even . . . farmyard hens, on fashionable bonnets before I die."

The biggest obstacle to halting the plume trade was, as it had always been, economic. Fashion, both here and abroad, dictated that bird plumes be used on ladies' bonnets, and even sympathetic milliners who might like to get out of the plume trade altogether could ignore this demand only at their own financial peril. Plumes were worth their weight in gold. Nevertheless, neither the AOU Committee on the Protection of North American Birds nor the Audubon Societies gave up the fight against the millinery trade. They fought for stronger state laws and urged that women abstain from purchasing plumed hats. At one point society members tried to wean women from this fashion by suggesting

that they wear Audubonetts, hats decked out in colorful ribbons and other items unrelated to birds, but these alternative chapeaux never caught on. Milliners often viciously and sometimes humorously attacked the "extremists" of the Audubon Societies. In one advertisement of the time, a milliner on Long Island offered for sale not only traditional plumed hats but also the following for special customers: "To our kind and feeling friends who are prejudiced against the wearing of birds, besides such as are protected by law, we respectfully offer a fine selection of FISH of different breeds, which are the latest Parisian creation."

Florida was one of the places where the fight to save the plume birds was most intense, and for good reason. It was home to perhaps the largest populations of plume birds in the United States and the largest population of plume hunters. One of those hunters was Guy Bradley, who, with his friend Charles William Pierce, took a Frenchman by the name of Chevalier on

LEFT: Saguaro cactus at sunset at the Kofa NWR, Arizona.

Green-backed heron searching for food at the Arthur R. Marshall Loxahatchee NWR, Florida.

an expedition in southern Florida in the spring of 1885. Pierce kept a journal of the trip.

Mr. Chevalier is a naturalist and we are going on a bird-collecting trip. Pelican skins are the main object of the trip, plumes next, also cormorants skins, in fact all kinds of birds. Mr. Chevalier has a market for them in Paris. He gets fifty cents for the pelican skins, twenty-five cents for sea swallows or the least tern, $10 for great white heron, and $25 for flamingo skins. Great white herons are scarce, and flamingos more so. If it was not for that we would soon make the old man rich.

The plight of the birds in Florida was trumpeted nationwide and became a source of much debate and concern. The September 1887 issue of

Legislators in Florida were well aware that they had a problem. In 1877 Florida passed legislation to prevent the destruction of the plume-bird nests, eggs, and juveniles. Feather merchants and market hunters, a powerful combination in local politics, got the law repealed two years later. In 1891 another law was passed; this one forbade the killing of birds to sell their plumes. As expected in a state as large and wild as Florida was at the time, enforcement of this new law was dubious at best. In 1897 the legislature gave the governor the power to appoint game wardens. Enforcement improved, but it was still spotty. Then in 1901 the AOU lobbied successfully to get the Florida legislature to pass the Model Law. William Dutcher and Theodore Palmer spearheaded this effort. Dutcher was a charter member of the AOU bird committee and a moving force in the fledgling National Committee of the Audubon Societies of America, of which he became the first chairman. Palmer was an assistant chief of the Division of Biological Survey and also a member of the bird committee.

With the Model Law in place, the AOU began hiring and paying for extra wardens in key locations throughout Florida where bird colonies were most threatened. Beginning in 1900 the financing for these hires came from the "Thayer" fund, monies solicited by Abbott Thayer, a New York artist and avid bird protectionist, and made available to the bird committee. One of the first wardens hired in this manner was reformed plume hunter Guy Bradley. In commenting on Bradley's nomination to the post, a member of the Florida Audubon Society stated that, although Bradley "was a thorough woodsman, a plume hunter by occupation before the

Grinnell's ill-fated *Audubon Magazine* ran an article on the situation in Florida that ended with the following fiery indictment: "A war of extermination against these birds is a war against God and Nature, and reflects no less discredit on the government which tolerates it supinely, than on the individuals who prosecute it for gain."

LEFT: Clouds reflecting in a desert spring–fed marsh at the Fish Springs NWR, Utah.

Endangered Lange's metalmark butterfly on naked buckwheat at the Antioch Dunes NWR, California.

An endangered brown pelican at the Pelican Island NWR, Florida.

RIGHT: The Illinois River meandering through the Arapaho NWR, Colorado.

passage of the present law, since which time, as I have ample testimony, he has not killed a bird. . . . I know of no better man for game warden in the whole state of Florida than Guy."

Pelican Island was another location where the AOU wanted to place a warden. It was a small island, roughly 5 acres, located on the east coast of Florida, across from the small village of Sebastian, about 135 miles north of Miami. For many years ornithologists and birdwatchers had visited the island, which played host to between two thousand and three thousand brown pelicans and was well-known as the only breeding site of these birds on the Atlantic Coast. One of those visitors was Frank M. Chapman, the curator of ornithology at the American Museum of Natural

History and actively involved in the AOU and the Audubon Societies. On his honeymoon in 1898, Chapman had visited Pelican Island and declared it "by far the most fascinating place it has ever been my fortune to see in the world of birds." Two years later, Chapman returned to see how the island's pelican population had fared. He was greatly disappointed. "I regret to say, that the population of the island has decreased." He then made a plea for preservation.

> The island is very accessible, the Florida law affords Pelicans no protection, and a party of quill-hunters might easily kill practically all the inhabitants of Pelican Island within a few days. The loss would be irreparable, and, it is to be especially noted, would not be confined to the vicinity, but would affect the whole east coast of Florida . . . if the natives of the state ever open their eyes to the

indisputable fact that a living bird is of incalculably greater value to them than a dead one, they may perhaps take some steps to defend their rights, and by passing and enforcing proper laws, put an end to the devastations of the northern plume agents, who have robbed their state of one of its greatest charms.

Chapman's plea was printed in *Bird-Lore,* a magazine that he had launched in 1899 with the intent of binding together the various Audubon Societies nationwide through the written word. *Bird-Lore* was an impressive successor to the original *Audubon Magazine* and would morph nearly forty years later into *Audubon.* At the suggestion of Chapman, Dutcher wrote to F. E. B. "Ma" Latham in March 1902 to find a suitable warden for Pelican Island. Ma Latham and her husband, Charles, ran Oak Lodge, a boardinghouse about 9 miles up the Indian River from the island. Over the years the lodge had become a base of

operations for scientists, artists, and naturalists intent on documenting the natural history of the state. Chapman had stayed there and knew of Ma Latham's keen interest in protecting wildlife and her extensive knowledge of the area. If anyone could recommend a solid warden for Pelican Island, it would be Ma Latham. She, in turn, interviewed Paul Kroegel for the job in April of that year. The AOU hired him, paying him $50 to protect the birds during the roughly six-month nesting season.

Kroegel was the son of a German immigrant and a resident boat builder in Sebastian, Florida, who lived within sight of Pelican Island, which was about 2 miles offshore from his house. He was born in 1864 in Chemnitz, Germany, and moved with his father and brother to Chicago at the age of six. About ten years later, his family moved to Florida. A slight man with blue eyes

and an impressively large walrus mustache, Kroegel had developed a strong attachment to the pelicans in part, he would later say, because his difficult childhood had steeled his resolve to do important things with his life and one of those things was protecting wildlife. For years Kroegel had witnessed the depredations of

Broad-winged hawk migrating through the Noxubee NWR, Mississippi.

plume hunters and the slaughter of pelicans by boaters who passed by the island and shot the birds for sport. Dr. James Henshall recorded the senselessness of the latter activity in his 1884 book, *Camping and Cruising in Florida.* In a section on Pelican Island, he wrote, "As we passed we saw a party of northern tourists at the island, shooting down the harmless birds by the scores through mere wantonness. As volley after volley came booming over the water, we felt quite disgusted at the useless slaughter, and bore away as soon as possible and entered the narrows."

Even before Kroegel was retained as warden, the AOU had begun exploring the possibility of purchasing Pelican Island. Chapman first raised the idea sometime in 1900. Then in his report for 1902 to the AOU, Dutcher wrote,

> As it is important that this colony should always be protected, it has been deemed advisable to get legal possession of it, and to that end your Committee has had it surveyed and has taken all the necessary steps to purchase the island. . . . It is

hoped that before the next breeding season is reached the A.O.U. will have absolute control of the island as owner in fee simple.

However, it soon became apparent that purchasing the island was not a simple task. Among the obstacles were bureaucratic red tape and the legality of transferring federal public lands to private ownership other than through the Homesteading Act. In February 1903 Dutcher wrote to Palmer, asking him to help move the purchase forward. "Will it not be possible for you . . . to go to . . . Interior, in order to hurry up the Pelican Island matter?" Dutcher wrote again a short time later, expressing his continuing concerns about the delays in resolving this matter. Palmer responded on February 21. He noted the many difficulties inherent in the transfer process, then ended the letter with a new idea—"Still another solution of the question is to have the island set apart as a government reserve. I find that we can have this done by executive order at short notice, and if the request is made before any claims are filed it will effectually shut out all comers." On February 26 Dutcher drafted a letter to the secretary of agriculture requesting that Pelican Island be set aside as a reserve. The secretary drafted his own letter to that effect and, attaching Dutcher's letter, forwarded the package to the secretary of the interior, urging that action be taken to protect the island. Within a few weeks this idea had percolated up to President Theodore Roosevelt, who reportedly asked one of his assistants, "is there any law that will prevent me from declaring Pelican Island a federal bird reservation." Upon hearing that there was not, Roosevelt said, "very well, then I so declare it," and on March 14, 1903, he signed the executive order creating the Pelican Island Reservation, the first of all the refuges established in what was to ultimately become the National Wildlife Refuge System. Whereas Roosevelt's action officially gave birth to the refuge system, much of the credit for launching the refuge system must be shared with the untold number of individuals and organizations whose stories are recounted in the preceding pages. Their efforts laid the groundwork for Roosevelt to act and were integral to the evolution of the refuge system—a process that continues today.

About three weeks after Roosevelt signed the executive order, Kroegel received a letter from Washington with the joyous news that he had been "appointed warden in charge of Pelican Island Reservation . . . in the Division of Biological Survey, in the United States Department of Agriculture, at the rate of one dollar per month." Since Congress failed to appropriate any money for Kroegel's employment, the AOU continued its practice of pay-

ing his salary. The Division of Biological Survey and the AOU asked Kroegel to post two large signs on the island to identify it as a government preserve and to warn off hunters. Soon after the signs went up, the pelicans vacated the island and nested on other islands nearby. When Chapman visited the next spring, he was alarmed by the desertion. Kroegel offered that perhaps the large signs had scared them off, and Chapman and Kroegel decided that they should be replaced by a group of smaller signs. Kroegel made the switch, and the birds returned soon thereafter. For similar reasons, when the Department of Agriculture sent him an enormous American flag to fly over the island, Kroegel instead put it on a flagpole near his dock.

Kroegel took his job very seriously and had many meals interrupted by the need to race to his boat and get out to the island to protect his avian wards. His daughter recalled, "Whenever

LEFT: This portrait of Theodore Roosevelt was taken on February 24, 1903, less than a month before he would sign the executive order establishing the Pelican Island NWR. Years later, he would write, "I am happy to say that I have been able to set aside in various parts of the country small, well-chosen tracts of ground to serve as sanctuaries and nurseries for wild creatures." *Library of Congress.*

Paul Kroegel with one of his beloved pelicans. *U.S. Fish and Wildlife Service.*

Skimmer dragonfly at the Santa Ana NWR, Texas.

RIGHT: An ephemeral playa lake at the Bitter Lake NWR, New Mexico.

boats would come down the river, they would always blow their whistles to salute the flag. That gave him his warning and when he heard a boat whistle he would jump up and get to the river and sail his boat to the island. It's a wonder he didn't die of ulcers." Being a warden was a dangerous job. Kroegel often had to confront armed market hunters who were in no mood to be told they couldn't pursue their livelihood. Kroegel was up to the task. "When diplomacy and dignified authority were ignored," his daughter said, "he reached for his double-barreled ten-gauge shotgun, which he always carried in his boat, and chased the invaders away from the area."

The danger inherent in the simple act of protecting birds was made tragically apparent in the case of Guy Bradley, a friend of Kroegel's. Working as an Audubon Society warden along Florida's southeastern coast, Bradley often faced dangerous situations confronting plume hunters, but he knew his adversaries well, having been a successful plume hunter himself earlier in life, and by all accounts he performed his job admirably. Bradley would make his rounds on the *Audubon,* a motorboat purchased for him by the Florida Audubon Society and built by Kroegel.

On July 8, 1905, Bradley looked out from the porch of his cottage across Florida Bay and noticed a boat moving toward a small island called Oyster Key, home to a variety of plume birds. Witnesses later testified that Bradley got in his boat and went to investigate. The boat Bradley had gone to check on belonged to Walter Smith, whose son had reportedly been arrested before by Bradley for killing plume birds. Based on later testimony of Smith and other witnesses on Smith's boat, Bradley had come to arrest Smith's son. Smith asked Bradley if he had a warrant, whereupon Bradley told him

a warrant wasn't needed when someone was caught committing a crime. "Well," Smith said while grabbing his rifle, "if you want him you have to come aboard of this boat and take him." Bradley responded, "Put down that rifle, and I will come aboard." According to Smith, Bradley shot at him but missed. Smith shot back and hit Bradley, who collapsed in his boat. Rather than check on Bradley's condition, Smith sailed away and left the *Audubon* drifting.

Smith was brought up on murder charges, but they were eventually dropped even though the evidence presented during the trial pointed strongly in the direction of his guilt, including testimony that Bradley, purported to be an excellent marksman, had never fired his weapon. Dutcher was incensed by the verdict and wrote an article in *Bird-Lore* condemning it.

> A home broken up, children left fatherless, a woman widowed and sorrowing, a faithful and devoted warden, who was a young and sturdy man, cut off in a moment, and for what? That a few more plume birds might be secured to adorn heartless women's bonnets. Heretofore the price has been the life of the birds, now is added human blood.

Bradley was buried on a ridge overlooking the ocean. His boat, the *Audubon,* was returned to Kroegel, who used it to patrol Pelican Island. *Collier's Weekly* labeled Bradley "Bird Protection's First Martyr." Unfortunately, he wouldn't be the last. Game wardens up through the present have often put their lives on the line, and some have given the ultimate sacrifice. Kroegel was able to avoid this fate. He served as Pelican Island's game warden until 1926, when

the government, pointing out that the pelicans had abandoned the island, decided his services were no longer needed (the pelicans later returned). Kroegel's daughter claimed that President "Calvin Coolidge got rid of him for stingy purposes!" noting that at the time of his retirement his federal salary had been hiked to $15 a month.

Kroegel died at the age of 84 in 1948. On November 14, 1963, the National Park Service bestowed a great honor on Pelican Island by making it the first wildlife area to be designated as a Registered National Historic Landmark. The honor was accorded after National Park Service historians and outside scholars concluded that Pelican Island possessed "exceptional value in commemorating or illustrating the history of the United States." Over the years additions of land have increased the size of the Pelican Island NWR to 5,278 acres, a far cry from its humble beginnings.

5

THEODORE ROOSEVELT—
A FORCE OF AND FOR NATURE

Theodore Roosevelt's concern for the pelicans and his establishment of the Pelican Island Reservation were not the least bit surprising. The man who would earn the moniker "the Conservation President" had loved nature and wildlife for most of his life. As a sickly child who had to spend considerable time indoors, he sought comfort in the books in his parents' library, including books on wildlife that captured his imagination. When he got a little older and less frail, Roosevelt searched for animals to study in the woods around his parents' house. At the age of seven, he launched the "Roosevelt Museum of Natural History," replete with shells, skulls, nests, eggs, and rocks. Not too long after, he learned taxidermy and used his first gun to add to his collection of stuffed animals. Frank M. Chapman later noted that, for his age, he was "a very promising taxidermist." Some of his handiwork can still be seen in the halls of the American Museum of Natural History, where Chapman was once curator of ornithology.

Hardwood forest in the mist at the Cypress Creek NWR, Illinois.

Roosevelt went to Harvard University to study natural history and become, he said, "a scientific man." He was a dashing figure on

51

campus, driving his dogcart to and from classes and sporting muttonchops. The study in his dormitory suite was full of animals, both dead and alive. Toward the end of his stay at Harvard, he abruptly changed his professional aspirations, leaving natural history for the study of politics with hopes of a career in law or public affairs. There has been much speculation on the reason for Roosevelt's change of heart. Some have argued that he did so at the request of his future wife, Alice Lee, who perhaps thought natural history was not a proper career for her intended. Others look to his family, few of whom encouraged his pursuit of science, at least as a basis for choosing a profession. Roosevelt himself said that his new direction had nothing to do with either Alice or his family but rather Harvard's training in natural history, which, to Roosevelt's thinking, focused too much on microscopes, tissues, and dead animals and not enough on the living, breathing natural world of the great outdoors.

Although Roosevelt chose politics over science, his deep connection with and respect for nature greatly affected the rest of his professional life. As governor of New York, he urged the state to forbid factories from turning bird skins into adornment, arguing that live birds in their element were infinitely more beautiful than dead birds upon women's hats. Also as governor he wrote a letter to Chapman that gave voice to his deep concern for the avian world.

> I would like to see all the harmless wild things, but especially all birds, protected in every way. I do not understand how any man or woman who really loves nature can fail to try to exert all influence in support of such objects as those of the Audubon Society. . . . The destruction of the Wild Pigeon and the Carolina Paroquet has meant a loss as severe as if the Catskills and the Palisades were taken away. When I hear of the destruction of a species I feel as if all the works of some great writer had perished.

As president, too, Roosevelt often spoke of and wrote about the need to protect birds. On July 18, 1906, he wrote a letter to William Dutcher expressing his concerns about the plume trade.

> Permit me on behalf of both Mrs. Roosevelt and myself to say how heartily we sympathize, not only with the work of the Audubon Societies generally, but particularly in their efforts to stop the sale and use of the so-called "aigrettes"—the plumes of the white herons. If anything, Mrs. Roosevelt feels even more strongly than I do on the matter.

Celebrated natural history writer John Burroughs said of Roosevelt, "I can not now recall that I have ever met a man with a keener and a more comprehensive interest in the wild life about us—an interest that is at once scientific and thoroughly human." When Roosevelt was asked later in life why he had such strong feelings for nature, he said, "I can no more

LEFT, ABOVE: **Black-shouldered kite feeding prey to young at the Laguna Atascosa NWR, Texas.**

LEFT, BELOW: **American coot feeding young at the Kern NWR, California.**

Blacktail prairie dog at the Wichita Mountains Wildlife Refuge, Oklahoma.

explain why I like 'natural history' than why I
like California canned peaches."

During his two terms as president, Roosevelt
often seemed most animated when in the company of naturalists or while experiencing nature
himself. In the spring of 1903, he made a political tour of the West but made sure to carve out
plenty of time for communing with nature. In
April he took a fifteen-day trip through
Yellowstone National Park, during which he
excluded the pack of reporters that had been
accompanying him. At the end of his stay,
Roosevelt declared the park a "veritable wonder-
land." In a later account of those days, Roosevelt
offered signs of his still-evolving philosophy on
humankind's relationship with the natural world.

> Every man who appreciates the majesty and beauty
> of the wilderness and of wild life, should strike
> hands with the far-sighted men who wish to pre-
> serve our material resources, in the effort to keep
> our forests and game-beasts, game-birds, and game-
> fish—indeed, all the living creatures of prairie and
> woodland and seashore—from wanton destruction.

A few weeks after leaving
Yellowstone, Roosevelt again
diverged from his political
rounds to spend time in
Yosemite National Park. Well
in advance of his trip,
Roosevelt had asked John
Muir to be his guide. "I want
to drop politics absolutely for
four days," Roosevelt wrote
to Muir, "and just be out in
the open with you." A better
choice could not have been
made. There was not a man
alive who knew more about
Yosemite than Muir, or who
fought more passionately for
its protection. Roosevelt was
dismayed to learn that Muir
had almost no interest in
birds and little facility for
identifying species by their
songs. "The hermit thrushes
meant nothing to him,"
Roosevelt later noted, "the
trees and the flowers and the
cliffs everything." Despite
this divergence in interests,
they got along well, each
focusing on what he knew
best. Muir was surprised, he
said, that Roosevelt was so
knowledgeable about natural history. Muir
added, "I never before had so interesting, hearty,
and manly a companion. I fairly fell in love with
him." The first night in Yosemite, Muir laid out
a bed of evergreen branches for Roosevelt to
sleep on. The next evening, the two of them
camped out on Glacier Point and awoke the following morning blanketed in 4 inches of freshly
fallen snow. When Roosevelt descended from

the heights of Yosemite that day he declared, "I never felt better in my life!"

The creation of the Pelican Island Reservation was just a start for Roosevelt. Over the remainder of his presidency, he repeatedly used his executive powers to set aside bird refuges. One of the most spectacular was the Klamath Lake Reservation, established in 1908, which protected not only colonial nesting birds but also very large populations of waterfowl, including ducks, geese, and swans. The Klamath Basin, which straddles the border between California and Oregon, is a major nesting area and is especially vital as a stopping off point for millions of migratory waterfowl. When explorers and then settlers came to this land, the numbers of ducks that carpeted the landscape amazed them. The hunters that came didn't just gaze at the ducks; they also started shooting them. By the late

The rocky oceanside cliffs at the Cape Mears NWR, Oregon.

1800s ducks by the trainload were being shipped out to destinations nationwide. One company shipped out about one hundred thousand ducks in a single season. Hunting, however, was only one of the pressures bearing down on the ducks in this area. The flatness of the land combined with its great fertility brought eager farmers who transformed the landscape and, in the process, gobbled up duck habitat. Roosevelt established the Klamath Lake Reservation at the urging of the National Association of Audubon Societies, the Oregon Audubon Society, and famed wildlife photographer William Finley, all of whom were worried that, if not for government action, this phenomenal area and its awe-inspiring concentrations of waterfowl would become a memory.

All of the refuges were placed under the supervision of the Division of Biological Survey, which was elevated in 1905 to be the Bureau of Biological Survey. In nearly all instances Roosevelt first learned about potential refuges from Audubon Society members who were encouraged by their leadership to keep an eye out for suitable lands that the government might set aside. In a 1908 issue of *Bird-Lore,* Dutcher urged his members on.

> There should be no limitation to the activities of members of this Association in seeking new tracts that can be set aside as bird refuges. . . . This is an important work that can be carried on by any member, and, in view of the fact that the nesting localities of ducks and shorebirds in all parts of the country are being rapidly restricted, it is important that refuges should be made where they still breed, in order to prevent extermination.

The Audubon Societies not only continued to identify potential bird refuges but also took on the responsibility for paying for the services of many refuge wardens, a practice that only began to be phased out many years later when Congress began to fulfill its financial responsibility. After leaving the White House, Roosevelt

reflected on the importance of game wardens, stating, "In Florida one of the best game wardens of the Audubon Society was killed by these sordid butchers [the plume hunters and eggers]. A fearless man and a good boat are needed to keep . . . [them] in awe." As for the paltry salary paid to wardens, he added, "The government pays many of its servants, usually those with rather easy jobs, too much; but the best men, who do the hardest work, the men in the life-saving and lighthouse service, the forest-rangers, and those who patrol and protect the reserves of wildlife, are almost always underpaid."

Soon after the first refuges were set aside, Representative John F. Lacey again enlisted in the cause of bird protection, introduced An Act to Protect Birds and Their Eggs in Game and Bird Preserves that was signed into law by Roosevelt on June 28, 1906. Before this, no federal law had specifically protected the birds on federal bird reservations. With the law in place, it was "unlawful for any person to hunt, trap, capture, wilfully disturb, or kill any bird of any kind or take the eggs of such birds" on any federal reservation. Violators could be imprisoned for six months, fined up to $500, or both.

Most of the bird refuges were relatively small, and many were uninhabited islands—in some cases just bare rock. In official pronouncements and informal conversation, people often referred to the refuges as "sterile tracts of land, worthless for other purposes" such as agriculture or logging. That may have been accurate as well as a political necessity, but these "worthless" pieces of land were of critical importance to the birds they were intended to protect. The plume trade was dying a slow death, as was the practice of egging. But the threats to birds were still very real.

The need for vigilance on refuges was made tragically clear in 1909 on the island of Laysan, which was part of the Hawaiian Islands

Young bull moose at the Lake Umbagog NWR, New Hampshire.

Laysan albatross with chick at the Kilauea Point NWR, Kauai, Hawaii.

Reservation created by Roosevelt earlier that year. In May foreign plume hunters landed on the island and laid into their work. By the fall, more than three hundred thousand albatrosses, as well as other birds, had been killed. This wave of destruction was brought to a halt by the arrival in January 1910 of the U.S. cutter *Thetis,* the crew of which arrested twenty-three poachers and took them to Honolulu along with the plumage they had readied for shipment to Japan. An American observer documented the inhu-

manity and cruelty of the hunters when he visited the island the next year. "In this dry cistern the living birds were kept by the hundreds to slowly starve to death. In this way the fatty tissue lying next to the skin was used up, leaving the skin quite free from grease, so that when they were prepared [for market] little or no cleaning was necessary."

However beneficial the bird reservations were, not everyone approved of the way in which Roosevelt established them. Some of his contemporaries viewed his liberal use of executive orders to set aside public lands as antidemocratic in that it was done without the consent of Congress. The area in which opposition to Roosevelt's tactics was most intense centered on forests. With a stroke of his pen, Roosevelt, working closely with his chief forester, Gifford Pinchot, set aside vast forest reserves that would later become national forests. With respect to the use of executive orders to set aside bird reservations, the reaction was also intense. Roosevelt's most outspoken critic on this topic was F. W. Mondell, a congressman from Wyoming and member and later chairman of the Committee on Public Lands. In response to an executive order establishing the Loch-Katrine Bird Reservation in Mondell's home state, the congressman inserted into the February 11, 1909, *Congressional Record* a letter he had written on the subject to the head of the Bureau of Biological Survey. It concluded with the following pronouncement: "I desire to dissent most emphatically . . . and to register my protest against the order in question, or any like orders, as being without authority of law, beyond and in excess of executive authority, in violation of the rights of the States and their citizens, and in direct conflict with the decisions of the Supreme Court of the United States." On the same day Mondell took to the floor of the House and sounded the alarm. "If this practice is to continue, there is no telling how many bird preserves we may have or how much of the territory of the Union these federal bird preserves may ultimately cover. If the Executive may create 26 preserves in various states [the number at the time], he can create 2,600."

Given Mondell's perspective on the issue, he must have been absolutely apoplectic two weeks later when Roosevelt established seventeen more bird reservations by executive order. It was part of Roosevelt's midnight rush of executive orders prior to his relinquishing the presidency to

William Howard Taft on March 4, 1909. And he wasn't done yet. On February 27 Roosevelt added seven more bird reservations. Finally, on March 2, almost as he was walking out the door, Roosevelt capped his effort with an order creating Bogoslof Bird Reservation in Alaska. Through the power of his pen, Roosevelt had established fifty-one bird reservations in seventeen states and three territories. Mondell's claims and fears notwithstanding, Roosevelt's use of his executive powers to establish reservations was never seriously challenged. In his autobiography, penned in 1913, Roosevelt offered his perspective on the use of presidential powers to set aside public lands. "I acted on the theory that the President could at any time in his discretion withdraw from entry any of the public land of the United States and reserve the same for . . . public purposes." In 1915 Roosevelt's boldness was legally vindicated by a Supreme Court ruling that, although it didn't turn on the question of setting aside bird reservations, clearly stated that the president had the authority to reserve government lands for public purposes. If there was any doubt that this ruling applied to bird reservations, the court eliminated it by citing the establishment of such reservations as a proper use of executive authority.

Roosevelt wasn't only concerned about birds. His intimate connection with big game led him to wield his powers for their protection as well. On January 24, 1905, Roosevelt signed a law that gave him the power to set aside parts of the Wichita National Forest Reserve in Oklahoma for the protection of game animals and birds. Soon thereafter he officially renamed the forest reserve the Wichita National Forest and Game Preserve (in 1935 the reserve was transferred from the U.S. Forest Service to the Bureau of Biological Survey and became part of the refuge system). During testimony in favor of the law,

One of the bison donated by the New York Zoological Society in a crate for the long train ride to the Wichita National Forest Reserve in Oklahoma. *Library of Congress.*

RIGHT: Bison with calf at the National Bison Range, Montana.

the New York Zoological Society had offered to donate fifteen of its bison to serve as breeding stock for the reserve. The man behind this offer was Dr. William T. Hornaday, the director of the New York Zoological Society, one of the founders of the American Bison Society, and a major force in the world of wildlife protection. He had long railed against the failure of government to protect the bison when there were still significant numbers of them to protect. In an article in *Cosmopolitan* in 1886, Hornaday derided the too-little-too-late protection efforts in the West. "While the territories are passing laws against the killing of the buffalo, they ought also, by all means, make the killing of Mastodons between August 15th and December 1 punishable by fine or imprisonment."

The New York Zoological Society kept its end of the bargain, providing fifteen bison for the new game reserve. Frank Rush, a U.S. Forest Service superintendent from Oklahoma, oversaw the shipment and recorded his observations. "On October 11, 1907, 15 of the best buffaloes in the New York Zoological Park were put in crates

(each one occupying a separate crate) and started for Cache, Oklahoma. On October 18 they were liberated in the buffalo yards at Forest Headquarters, after being sprayed with crude oil to prevent ticks from getting to them."

Three years later, in 1908, Roosevelt signed a bill establishing the National Bison Range on the Flathead Indian Reservation, north of Missoula, Montana. This was a major step forward for the fledgling refuge system because it represented the first time that Congress had appropriated funds ($30,000) to purchase refuge lands—in this case to pay the Native Americans for their land (an additional $10,000 was appropriated to pay for fencing). This time the American Bison Society stocked the new refuge with thirty-four animals that it had purchased for this purpose.

When Roosevelt left office, he could look back on an amazing record of accomplishments in the field of conservation. In 1911 Senator Robert LaFollette summed it up as follows: "When the historian of the future shall speak of Theodore Roosevelt, he is likely to say that he did many notable things, but that his greatest work was inspiring and actually beginning a world movement for staying territorial waste and saving for the human race the things on which alone a peaceful, progressive, and happy life can be founded."

History has proven LaFollette correct. Roosevelt's role in the creation of the refuge system should rank as one his most important conservation achievements. He was the right man at the right time, and his bold actions set the refuge system on its legs. In his autobiography Roosevelt reflected on the extremely "important . . . steps [he took] to preserve from destruction beautiful and wonderful wild creatures whose existence was threatened by greed and wantonness." He claimed that during his tenure "more was accomplished for the protection of

wild life in the United States than during all the previous years, excepting only the creation of Yellowstone National Park." He then launched into a long list of those accomplishments, including his establishment of the refuge system.

> The creation of these [fifty-one bird] reservations at once placed the United States in the front rank in the world work in bird protection. Among these reservations are the celebrated Pelican Island rookery . . . the extensive marshes bordering Klamath and Malheur Lakes in Oregon, formerly the scene of slaughter of ducks for market and ruthless destruction of plume birds for the millinery trade . . . and the great bird colonies on Laysan and sister islets in Hawaii, some of the greatest colonies of sea birds in the world.

Three years later, in his *Book-Lover's Holidays in the Open,* Roosevelt added,

> With the great majority of our most interesting and important wild birds and beasts the prime need is to protect them . . . especially by the creation of sanctuaries and refuges. . . . The progress made in the United States, of recent years, in creating and policing bird refuges, has been of capital importance. . . .
>
> . . . to lose the chance to see frigate-birds soaring in circles above the storm, or a file of pelicans winging their way homeward across the crimson afterglow of the sunset, or a myriad of terns flashing in the bright light of midday as they hover in a shifting maze above the beach—why, the loss is like the loss of a gallery of the masterpieces of the artists of old time.

GROWTH BY FITS AND STARTS

During the twenty years following Theodore Roosevelt's departure from the White House, the refuge system continued to grow. When he left office, the number of refuges stood at fifty-three (not including the Wichita National Forest and Game Preserve, which didn't become a refuge until 1935). In 1929 there were more than eighty. The total known acreage of all refuges in 1909 was 434,000. In 1929 it had risen to about five million, with nearly four million of that being attributable to just two refuges established in the wilds of Alaska. This relatively slow rate of growth did not reflect need. Continued threats to wildlife and the accumulating loss of habitat to progress made it increasingly important to preserve wild lands before it was too late. However, a lack of broad and deep public support for refuges, limited congressional appropriations for refuge purchases, and the absence of a leader like Roosevelt who took action into his own hands left the refuge system muddling along.

Eggs of an endangered least tern in a shallow nest at the Salt Plains NWR, Oklahoma.

Although the growth of the refuge system was not nearly as great as its supporters had hoped, the additions that were made in the second and

third decades of the twentieth century were of critical importance to wildlife. In 1912, Congress appropriated $45,000 to establish the National Elk Refuge in the vicinity of Jackson Hole, Wyoming. The elk, like the bison, is a grand animal with a troubled history. At one time elk were the most widely distributed of all deer species in North America. The first herds to succumb to hunting and the destruction of habitat were those in the East. By the late 1800s the only large herds were out West, but they too were increasingly pressured as humans carved up the elk's migration routes with ranches, farms, and fences and forced the animals into smaller and

Mounted in gold and hung from a watch fob, these teeth became the unofficial badge of the Benevolent and Protective Order of Elks, a fraternal service organization with millions of members. And many of those members commissioned necklaces of elk teeth for their wives. In the early 1900s, when the elk teeth trade hits its zenith, a pair of teeth could fetch from $10 to $25.

About this time some Wyoming residents became concerned about the survival of the elk. In 1906 D. C. Nowlin, the state's game warden, recommended establishing a refuge for the elk. The idea simmered for years as the elk's situation worsened. Meantime, the locals

smaller ranges. One sizeable herd that had traditionally traveled from Yellowstone National Park and the Grand Tetons to the wild hay meadows in the south soon found its route blocked by settlement and began stopping for the winter in and around Jackson Hole, a town of only sixty-four people in 1890, when the territory of Wyoming became a state.

Despite the scarcity of people in the Jackson Hole area, there were plenty of human-made dangers for the elk. Hunters in search of meat and trophies thinned the herds. Farmers competed for the land and didn't always look kindly upon elk eating the hay and forage that they had set aside for their animals. Perhaps the most pernicious of all the threats facing the elk were the tusk hunters who slaughtered the biggest of elk only to extract the animal's impressive canine teeth.

did what they could to help the elk survive. In the winter of 1906–1907, they fed hay, donated by the U.S. Forest Service and hauled by state game wardens, to a small group of snowbound elk to keep them from starving. In 1908 the state legislature asked Congress to grant the state five townships to be used for an elk refuge, but no grant was issued. That winter was especially bad. A resident at the time recalled, "Elk were dying all around us. There was a mass meeting in the clubhouse in town. Ranchers volunteered to donate hay and others donated their labor. Then they petitioned the governor for emergency relief for the elk." The residents of Jackson Hole were able to raise $1,000 to purchase hay and convinced the state legislature to add $5,000 to that. Despite these efforts nearly eight thousand elk died that winter —half of the entire herd. Continued harsh

winters, alternating with dry summers, reduced forage levels further, giving the elk little chance to hold their own, much less rebound. But the momentum was beginning to shift.

In 1911, Congress finally took heed of the calls from Wyoming and from concerned citizens throughout the nation and appropriated $20,000 to feed and protect the elk. The Bureau of Biological Survey was given responsibility for administering the money, and it sent biologist E. A. Preble to Jackson Hole to assess the situation. His evaluation of the dire situation prompted Congress to establish the National Elk Refuge, and Nowlin had the honor of being appointed the refuge's first warden.

The same bill that launched the National Elk Refuge gave life to the Wind Cave Game Preserve in South Dakota, which was intended to provide a range for another herd of bison donated by the American Bison Society. In fall 1912 an executive order established the Fort Niobrara Game Preserve on an abandoned military reservation in Nebraska, and two years later, the Sullys Hill Game Preserve was set aside in North Dakota. Both of these, like Wind Cave, were intended to benefit big game, including bison, elk, antelope, and deer.

On June 7, 1924, President Calvin Coolidge signed the bill creating the Upper Mississippi National Wild Life and Fish Refuge, a massive piece of real estate stretching over 300 miles of bottomlands along the river. Congress appropriated an impressive $1.5 million to purchase the refuge, which was different from other refuges in that it allowed for fishing and hunting. The driving force behind the refuge's creation was Will H. Dilg. A successful Chicago advertising man, Dilg had fished the upper Mississippi for decades and once remarked, "since boyhood the call of black bass waters has been my chief weakness." In early 1922 he joined fifty-four other fishermen

and hunters for lunch at the Chicago Athletic Association. All of the men were concerned that mounting threats to wildlife were diminishing their opportunities to fish and hunt. The idea of forming a new conservation group was raised, and by March the Izaak Walton League, named for the patron saint of sport fishermen, was up and running with Dilg as its president.

Dilg quit his advertising job and pursued his new position with zeal. Some felt that Dilg's intense drive to found the Izaak Walton League and fight for wildlife drew strength from his grief at having lost his young son on a fishing trip when the boy fell into the Mississippi and drowned. Whatever his motivations, Dilg was a powerful force for conservation. "I am weary of civilization's madness," he said, "and I yearn for the harmonious gladness of the woods and of the streams." In the summer of 1923, Dilg heard of a plan to drain and develop a huge swath of upper Mississippi bottomlands. "Why not," he countered, "turn the whole upper region into a great refuge?" A friend of Dilg's told him that his chances of convincing the federal government to do so were "not quite so thick as tissue paper." This did not deter Dilg. He sprang into action and used the Izaak Walton League's growing strength, along with his own persuasive powers, as a battering ram.

Dilg wangled a short meeting with Coolidge and made his case. The president was impressed and promised to sign the bill if Dilg could get it through Congress. With key congressmen as allies, and the support of other national groups, such as the two-million-member General Federation of Women's Clubs, Dilg settled into a room at the Willard Hotel in Washington, D.C., from which he directed an impressive lobbying campaign. A colleague reported that Dilg "had a staff of assistants, he had many callers, his messengers constantly came and went. He conducted

Longhorn cattle at the Fort Niobrara NWR, Nebraska.

Canyon tree frog at the Buenos Aires NWR, Arizona.

RIGHT: Western sandpipers and dunlins congregating during spring migration at the Gray's Harbor NWR, Washington.

his campaign on an expensive scale heretofore unknown in conservation circles." A bill to create the refuge made it through the House but hit a snag in the Senate. For some extra arm-twisting muscle, Dilg turned to Herbert Hoover, the secretary of commerce and an avid angler. Dilg and Hoover went to see Coolidge, who approved the use of a parliamentary procedure to force a vote, whereupon the bill passed. After Coolidge signed the bill, Dilg exclaimed, "At last the God of Nature and the wild things WON."

On April 23, 1928, Congress authorized the Bear River Migratory Bird Refuge, located in a part of Utah that had long been recognized as magnificent resting and breeding grounds for birds. On September 3, 1843, Captain John C. Fremont visited the Bear River delta and reported, "The waterfowl made this morning a noise like thunder." That evening, he and his companions had "a delicious supper of ducks, geeses, and plover." A few years later Captain Howard Stansbury, on a visit to the area, noted that he "had seen large flocks of birds before, in various parts of the country, . . . but never did I behold anything like the immense numbers here congregated together." Like the Upper Mississippi Wild Life and Fish Refuge, the Bear River Migratory Bird Refuge was not an inviolate sanctuary. While a minimum of 60 percent of the refuge had to remain completely protected, the rest was authorized to be open to hunting.

Implicit in the establishment of refuges was the idea that they could grow if needed or, alternatively, they could be eliminated if they were no longer needed. During the first and second decades of the twentieth century, some refuges changed size or entirely disappeared. For example, the National Elk Refuge in 1912, at its inception, covered 1,760 acres. Soon after, Congress added another 1,000 acres. Then, in 1925, the Izaak Walton League initiated a national fundraising campaign to purchase more land for the elk in Jackson Hole, which were again threatened with starvation. The campaign raised $36,000, some of it from schoolchildren, which was used to purchase 1,760 acres that were, in turn, donated to the government. At the other extreme was the Yukon Delta Reservation that Roosevelt created by executive order toward the end of his second term. It was enormous, encompassing 8 million acres or more of Alaskan wilderness. In 1922, however, another executive order reversed Roosevelt's and let the lands revert back to the public domain. In explaining the rationale for this decision, the Bureau of Biological Survey said, "no useful purpose would be served in the continuation of this extensive reserve, for the reason that . . . this region is remote and of too marshy a character to be desirable for settlement and this fact protects the birds to a great extent although many are taken annually by the resident Eskimos for food purposes." In 1980, Congress established a number of refuges in Alaska, one of which was the reconstituted Yukon Delta Reservation that was increased in size. The process of adding to existing refuges continues up through the present. Ever since 1976 eliminating refuges has been an authority reserved solely by Congress, and the exercise of this authority is a rare occurrence.

7

LEGAL PROTECTION
FOR THE BIRDS

As the refuge system slowly expanded during the second and third decades of the twentieth century, statutory changes took place that would have an extensive impact on its future growth. The push for change began almost immediately after the passage of the Lacey Act in 1900. To many observers the main drawback of the act was that it merely enhanced the enforcement of disparate state laws and thereby perpetuated a patchwork approach; still no overarching federal law governed birds. Of particular concern were migratory birds that crossed numerous state borders on their annual travels north and south. With each move into a new jurisdiction, the level of protection the birds received was contingent upon a different law. Inconsistencies in the laws meant that the path used by the birds could determine their fate. And in some states the local laws didn't provide much protection at all.

In 1904 Congressman George Shiras III of Pennsylvania launched the first major salvo in the campaign to expand federal oversight of migratory birds. On December 4 of that year, he introduced "A Bill to Protect Migratory Birds of the

Endangered whooping cranes in flight at the Aransas NWR, Texas.

73

United States," which was intended to move the federal government from the periphery of migratory bird management to center stage. The bill proposed that "all wild geese, and wild swans, brant, wild ducks, snipe, plover, woodcock, rail, wild pigeons, and all other migratory game birds which do not remain permanently the entire year within the borders of any State or Territory shall hereafter be deemed to be within the custody and protection of the Government of the United States." The bill also required the establishment of closed seasons throughout the country to protect the birds when they were at their most vulnerable.

Shiras was an unusual politician. He was a renowned outdoorsman and naturalist who had pioneered the art of nighttime wildlife photography. He was coaxed into running for Congress by his political party, and having no interest in making this a profession, he served notice upon winning that he would not run again. Most surprisingly, he kept his word. It is fitting that this forthright individual with a background in natural history would submit such a bill. He had witnessed the continued depredations of market hunters and game hogs and could see that the Lacey Act would not suffice to protect migratory birds. However compelling its logic, Shiras's bill did not gain many political adherents, and it died with the end of both the congressional session and Shiras's congressional career.

But the seed was planted. Audubon Societies, the American Ornithologists Union, *Forest and Stream,* and other supporters of the increased protection of migratory birds continued lobbying for the federal approach embodied in Shiras's bill, but year after year similar bills were voted down. In 1912 the so-called Weeks-McLean Bill became the focus of attention. Much more far ranging than the earlier bills, it placed all migratory game and insectivorous birds as well as migratory songbirds under federal control and forbade the taking of them except as provided for by federal regulations.

This bill, too, engendered stiff opposition, and it appeared as if it would be defeated as well. But this time some of the bill's supporters came up with a winning, if somewhat deceptive, strategy. They attached the Weeks-McLean Bill as a rider to a much larger appropriations bill that was passed by both houses of Congress and was ultimately signed by President William Taft just before he left office. Taft certainly was unaware that the Weeks-McLean Bill was buried within the appropriation's bill. He was firmly opposed to the bill because he believed it was an unconstitutional infringement on state powers. Taft's anger at being duped was later revealed when a

sportsman friend of the ex-president commended him on having signed Weeks-McLean into law. Taft replied that had he known about the rider, he would have vetoed the entire bill.

The law was immediately attacked, both in Congress, where calls were made for its repeal, and through the courts, where litigation threatened to overturn it. In 1914 a federal court ruled the law unconstitutional because it interfered with states' rights. The ruling was appealed, but the supporters of Weeks-McClean, concerned that the appeal might fail, sought to achieve the law's goals through alternative means. Leading this effort was Senator Elihu Root of New York, who preferred an approach based on the president's uncontested right to enter into international treaties and proposed a resolution encouraging the president to establish treaties with other countries for the purpose of protecting migratory birds. The resolution passed on July 7, 1913.

On August 18, 1916, President Woodrow Wilson signed the Migratory Bird Treaty between the United States and Great Britain. The treaty was intended to save "from indiscriminate slaughter and . . . [to ensure] the preservation of such migratory birds as are useful to man or harmless." It prohibited the hunting of insectivorous birds, greatly restricted the taking of other nongame birds, and established open and closed seasons for game birds. The treaty also repealed the Weeks-McLean Law. Almost two years later Congress approved implementing legislation for the treaty, which went into effect on July 3, 1918, and was administered by the Bureau of Biological Survey. With the treaty in place and the Weeks-McLean Law repealed, the question of the law's legality

became moot, and the appeal of the earlier federal court ruling was dropped.

The treaty came under fire, primarily from states' rightists and market hunters. While none contested the president's constitutionally based power to enter into treaties, there was still some doubt as to whether that power extended to migratory birds. The only body that could definitively answer that question was the Supreme Court, and it did so in the case of *Missouri v. Holland,* in which the state sought to have the treaty overturned on the basis that it unconstitutionally usurped the state's right to regulate migratory birds within its borders. On April 19, 1920, Justice Oliver Wendell Holmes, writing for the majority and affirming the treaty, eloquently pointed out the weaknesses of the state's arguments:

> The state . . . founds its claim of exclusive authority upon an assertion of title to migratory birds. . . . To put the claim of the state upon title is to lean upon a slender reed. Wild birds are not in the possession of anyone . . . the whole foundation of the state's rights is the presence within their jurisdiction of birds that yesterday had not arrived, tomorrow may be in another state, and in a week a thousand miles away. . . . Here a national interest of very nearly the first magnitude is involved. It can be protected only by national action in concert with that of another power. . . . But for the treaty and the statute, there soon might be no birds for any powers to deal with. We see nothing in the Constitution which compels the government to sit by while a food supply is cut off and the protectors of our forests and of our crops are destroyed. It is not sufficient to rely upon the states. The reliance is vain.

The treaty promised a brighter future for migratory birds, but many people were concerned that if the situation didn't improve quickly, the birds wouldn't have much of a future. Although reliable statistics on migratory bird populations were not available at the time, there was a general sense that many species were still facing serious threats. For the new law to work, it had to

Canada geese at the Sand Lake NWR, South Dakota. On April 15, 1852, Henry David Thoreau wrote in his journal: "How indispensable our one or two flocks of [Canada] geese in spring and autumn. What would be a spring in which that sound was not heard? Coming to unlock the fetters of northern rivers. Those animal steamers of the air."

be enforced, yet in the years immediately after the treaty's passage, the Bureau of Biological Survey's budgets for implementing the treaty were meager, often less than the amount single states spent on waterfowl regulation. And some argued that even if the treaty were enforced, the liberal bag limits it allowed were not enough to adequately protect the birds.

At the same time other forces were at work threatening migratory birds. Increased U.S. farm production during World War I to support the war effort led to the draining of the wetlands waterfowl relied on during their annual migrations. The postwar era's peace and prosperity further transformed the landscape. The rapidly expanding population increased the demand for more farmland, houses, office buildings, and roads. Shortened workweeks and greater wealth meant more leisure time and the financial means to enjoy it. Many turned to outdoor pursuits, including hunting. By the early 1920s over four million state hunting licenses were being issued annually, a dramatic increase over the one and a half million that were issued in 1911. New roads and easier access to automobiles allowed hunters to travel farther than their predecessors, to more remote areas, and once they got there, they used better guns, giving them an added edge in the pursuit of quarry.

Many theories about what to do to save

Singing western meadowlark at the Medicine Lake NWR, Montana.

RIGHT: Belmore Browne's suggestion for the design of a federal hunting license, as it appeared in the April 1921 issue of the *Bulletin of the American Game Protective Association*. What is most interesting about this image is that it appeared nearly fourteen years before the federal duck stamp became a reality.

Smithsonian Book of National Wildlife Refuges

migratory waterfowl were debated, but the public soon focused on the creation of refuges and public shooting grounds. For years the Bureau of Biological Survey had been calling for more refuges to ensure healthy migratory waterfowl populations. Its report in 1917 stated that "Increased protected areas for breeding places for the migratory wild geese, ducks, cranes, swans... should be provided. Additional wildlife refuges along the paths of migration are needed in order to secure improved and equalized opportunities for shooting wild fowl for food and recreation." A significant number of sportsmen agreed that additional inviolate refuges were needed, but they also wanted the creation of public shooting grounds, lands where the public could hunt game. An editorial in the *Bulletin of the American Game Protective Association* offered a perspective shared by many hunters of the day.

> If the young men of the next generation are to enjoy from the country's wild life anything like the benefits derived by the present outdoor man, we must be the one to shoulder the burden and see that our thoughtlessness or selfishness does not allow us to squander that which we hold in trust.
>
> Public shooting grounds must be established for the rank and file of the gunners who cannot afford to belong to exclusive clubs. . . . With the public shooting grounds must come more reserves where the birds should have absolute protection, for as the country becomes more settled, shooting would become impossible without them.

Although support for more refuges and public shooting grounds was growing, the question of financing such lands remained. Few wanted to rely solely on piecemeal appropriations from Congress. But, if not from Congress's coffers, then from where? George A. Lawyer, chief U.S. game warden, came up with a novel idea that he discussed with game warden Ray Holland, of *Missouri v. Holland* fame. What if the federal government required hunters to purchase hunting stamps through the post office and used the

proceeds to purchase land? This would have the dual benefits of generating a revenue stream while not creating another burdensome bureaucracy. Lawyer wrote to Holland, "why not sell [hunting stamps] as the government is selling war savings stamps?"

In 1921, identical bills were introduced in the Senate and House "providing for establishing shooting grounds for the public . . . game refuges and breeding grounds, for protecting migratory birds, and requiring a Federal license to hunt them." The license, in the form of a stamp, would cost $1 and be purchased at post offices throughout the country. Proceeds would go toward acquiring public shooting grounds and adjacent inviolate bird refuges where hunting was forbidden.

Many organizations supported the bill, including the National Association of Audubon Societies, the Boone and Crockett Club, the U.S. Department of Agriculture, the Camp Fire Club of America, and the International Association of Game, Fish, and Conservation Commissioners. There were opponents as well. States' rights advocates decried the bill's reach. Congressman F. W. Mondell, perhaps still smarting from Roosevelt's liberal use of executive orders, argued that the bill was unconstitutional. "I believe the measure if so far-reaching in its consequences, would be so tremendously harmful in the long run to my country and to its people, that I can not bring myself to support it or any part of it." Others were opposed to the sale of stamps, arguing strenuously against this new "tax." The bill passed the Senate but fell short in the House.

Bureau of Biological Survey employee Frederick Lincoln banding a bird in the 1920s. Lincoln is often referred to as the father of waterfowl flyways in North America on account of his groundbreaking work on waterfowl migrations. An early proponent of using planes as a tool in waterfowl management, Lincoln conducted the first aerial census of wintering duck populations on January 25, 1935. *U.S. Fish and Wildlife Service.*

Sunrise on the Bitterroot Mountains at the Lee Metcalf NWR, Montana.

BELOW: Senator Peter Norbeck, of South Dakota, played a critical role in creating the Federal Duck Stamp Program. *U.S. Senate Historical Office.*

In subsequent years similar bills were introduced, but none passed. The most effective voice in opposition to these bills was William T. Hornaday's. He was a fiery, iconoclastic character who wielded a mighty voice and a mightier pen. He tried to discredit the bills and their supporters. The public shooting grounds provision was, to him, the equivalent of creating "slaughter pens" making it more convenient for hunters to kill migratory waterfowl. He called the supporters of the bills "game hogs," "butchers," and "the armies of destruction." The real supporters of the bills, Hornaday claimed, were the gun and ammunition companies who were only interested in selling more of their products. New York Senator Fiorella La Guardia echoed this concern, stating, "These lobbyists know that the sole purpose of...[these bills] is not to conserve birds but to slaughter birds and to create a better market for cartridges, powder, and guns."

As the legislative battle raged on, the status of waterfowl worsened. Writing in the mid-1920s, E. W. Nelson, chief of the Bureau of Biological Survey, urged immediate action. "The danger to the perpetualism of the stock of wildfowl is so great and so imminent . . . that there is the most vital need for all conservationists and lovers of wildlife to sink petty differences of opinions as to the details and unite in constructive work to insure the future of our migratory game birds."

Toward the end of 1920s Senator Peter Norbeck of South Dakota, a strong supporter of wildlife protection, offered a bill slightly different from those that had failed before. It included the stamp idea but would allow for hunting on refuges only when the secretary of agriculture found that it "would not endanger the future supply of birds." In the face of continued strong opposition to even the possibility of hunting on refuges, as well as the requirement that hunters

purchase a stamp, Norbeck stripped away the offending provisions to gain passage. The refuges would be "inviolate sanctuaries," and funding would have to come from the U.S. Treasury. Norbeck's strategy worked, and on February 18, 1929, President Hoover signed into law the Migratory Bird Conservation Act.

Secretary of Agriculture William Marion Jardine hailed the new law.

Without the Refuge Act to support the provisions of earlier Federal legislation it is difficult to conceive how our birds . . . could for long withstand or survive in satisfactory numbers the encroachment of industry and the losses sustained by indiscriminate shooting on practically every feeding ground in the country. . . . Americans may well call down blessings upon the heads of those whose love of nature, whose far-sightedness, and whose practical common sense generously exercised in the adjustment of a difficult problem have made a splendid law possible.

In 1934 Holland, then editor of *Field and Stream,* offered a different take on the event, saying, "the bill [with the shooting grounds provision] was defeated by a group of long-haired boys who called themselves conservationists. . . . Later, the bill was hamstrung, quartered and drawn" to guarantee passage.

8

DUCKS AND THE DUST BOWL

The passage of the Migratory Bird Conservation Act couldn't have come at a more critical time. By the Bureau of Biological Survey's own admission, any success achieved by years of regulations restricting the bag limits and open seasons for hunters would be lost unless waterfowl habitat was preserved. Each day valuable habitat succumbed to the march of development. Yet the new law had only middling results.

Hope for major funding of the new law was dashed with the crash of the stock market in October 1929. A country reeling from a financial meltdown had little interest in migratory waterfowl protection. Still, the refuge system did grow slowly in the early 1930s. Some of the migratory waterfowl refuges added during this time were Blackwater in Maryland, Swanquarter in North Carolina, and St. Marks in Florida. Even though the focus of activity was on migratory waterfowl, there was also some good news for other types of refuges.

Wintering mallards exploding off the water at the Wheeler NWR, Alabama.

On January 26, 1931, Hoover signed an executive order creating the Charles Sheldon National Antelope Refuge in Nevada. Antelope

Pronghorn antelope at the National Bison Range, Montana. Pronghorns are extremely fast runners, capable of reaching speeds of 50 miles per hour, and during short bursts, they can approach 60 miles per hour. Although these speedy animals are usually referred to as antelope, pronghorns are actually part of a uniquely American family of ruminants and are only distantly related to the true antelope that live in Africa, such as gazelles and impalas.

populations had long been in trouble from hunting and habitat destruction, and by the 1920s these once numerous animals were reduced to scattered pockets struggling to survive. In 1923 E. W. Nelson, chief of the Bureau of Biological Survey, called a meeting at the National Museum of Natural History in Washington, D.C., where a range of prominent conservation figures considered the plight of the antelope and what to do about it. Although a committee that met during the meeting crafted a bill establishing an antelope refuge in southeastern Oregon, nothing came of it. One person, however, would not let the issue drop. Worried about the fate of the antelope, E. R. Sans, a biologist for the Bureau of Biological Survey, had long been an ardent salesman for the refuge idea. In 1928 he took advantage of a golden opportunity. T. Gilbert Pearson, then president of the National Association of Audubon Societies, was making a trip to Reno to visit a pelican colony in nearby Anaho Lake, and Sans offered to take him there as long as Pearson promised to visit the antelope as well. Pearson agreed and returned east committed to helping the antelope refuge become a reality. He brought up the issue within the National Association of Audubon Societies and with the Boone and Crockett Club, of which he was a member. Then on September 21, 1928, Charles Sheldon, a longtime member of the club and close friend of Teddy Roosevelt's, died of a sudden heart attack while in Nova Scotia. Sheldon represented the club at the 1923 meeting at the National Museum of Natural History and was a strong supporter of the refuge idea. As a monument to Sheldon's memory, the Boone and Crockett Club raised $10,000 to purchase refuge habitat. Another $10,000 for the same purpose was raised by the National Association of Audubon Societies. Together this money purchased 119 acres of

privately owned land in Nevada, all of which was turned over to the federal government. Hoover signed the executive order soon after, bringing the total acreage of the refuge to 34,000. Although a valuable start, this land was not enough to adequately protect a population that traveled widely over three states. That situation was partly remedied in 1936, when President Franklin Delano Roosevelt, Theodore's fifth cousin, created the 549,000-acre Charles Sheldon Antelope Range, adjacent to the refuge, and also established the Hart Mountain National Antelope Refuge in Oregon.

Migratory waterfowl in the early 1930s were suffering from forces much more dangerous than a lack of funding. The Dust Bowl had begun. Year after year of low precipitation transformed vast stretches of the southern plains and the Great Plains into virtual deserts where the winds kicked up billowing black clouds of soil that roiled over the landscape and turned day into night. The resting, nesting, and feeding areas that migratory waterfowl relied on literally disappeared. Vast lakes were transformed into small ponds, rivers became streams or dry riverbeds, and small ponds and wetlands turned into cracked mud. In August 1931 President Hoover issued a proclamation on the conservation of waterfowl that limited the coming fall duck-hunting season to one month. Pearson commented that "Wild waterfowl in this country have recently passed through two very adverse breeding seasons and their numbers are less today than during the life time of any one present."

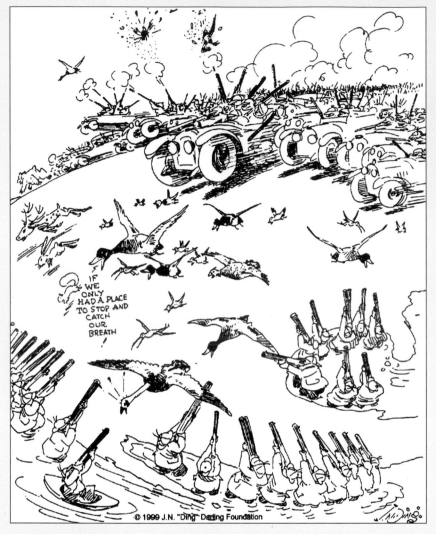

"IF WE ONLY HAD A PLACE TO STOP AND CATCH OUR BREATH!"

© 1999 J.N. "Ding" Darling Foundation

"Wanted: More and Better Game Refuges" (April 30, 1928) by Ding Darling. Darling ultimately won two Pulitzer prizes for his political cartoons. Conservation and the plight of migratory waterfowl were but two of the many topics that Darling commented on during his extremely prolific cartooning career. *Courtesy of the J. N. "Ding" Darling Foundation.*

RIGHT: Jay Norwood "Ding" Darling, 1876–1962. One of the giants of conservation, Darling rallied the forces for creating refuges through his cartoons and dynamic leadership. Reflecting on the plight of migratory waterfowl, Darling said, "Ducks don't nest on picket fences." *Courtesy of the J. N. "Ding" Darling Foundation.*

In the depths of the Great Depression and the Dust Bowl, the political fortunes of the refuge system took a sharp turn for the better. A national debate arose about what should be done to save the plummeting waterfowl populations. There were calls to kill crows, ban hunting, reduce bag limits dramatically, and raise ducks in captivity that could then be released into the wild. Jay Norwood "Ding" Darling, a Pulitzer prize–winning political cartoonist who had long penned cartoons urging better protection of waterfowl, observed that "the sportsmen's fraternity was as full of misinformation as a Soviet broadcast, and it quarreled over as many theories for salvation of the ducks as religionists over formulas for getting into heaven." But, as had been the case late in the second decade of the twentieth century and into the third, most argued for more refuges.

In January 1934 President Franklin Delano Roosevelt appointed the Committee on Wild-Life Restoration, sometimes referred to as the duck committee, to evaluate the situation and recommend a restoration plan that would benefit waterfowl as well as songbirds, shorebirds, mammals, and other animals. Its members were Thomas H. Beck, editor in chief of *Collier's Weekly* and an active conservationist; Darling; and Aldo Leopold, then professor of game management in the agricultural economics department at the University of Wisconsin, Madison. The *Chicago Tribune* reflected the optimism of many organizations nationwide when it predicted that out of the committee would come a "gigantic national project to increase game birds in this country . . . utilize 20 to 50 million acres . . . [and] increase healthful recreation for million[s] of outdoor fans." Roosevelt added to the anticipation by promising

$1 million to fund the committee's plan if it were approved.

Beck, Darling, and Leopold pursued their task with zeal, interviewing federal, state, and local wildlife managers, soliciting management suggestions, and identifying potential refuge lands. The committee didn't start from scratch. Its efforts built upon years of work by the Bureau of Biological Survey that documented wetland conditions across the country and mapped potential areas for refuge acquisition. Leopold commented on the importance of the committee's work in a private letter to Darling. "We must not delude ourselves by seeing this job as merely a heaven-sent chance to buy some lands. It is . . . the chance to make or break federal leadership in wildlife conservation." After five weeks of work, the committee attempted to write its report, and all hell broke loose. "If there is a word in the English language expressing violent explosion, only louder and longer lasting," Darling commented later, "I'd like to use it now." Beck wanted the report to say that the

Bureau of Biological Survey was "incompetent and unscientific" and should be abolished. Leopold, fed up with Beck's imperious manner and his conclusions, left for home. Darling's efforts to prepare an acceptable compromise report were only partially successful. In February the three submitted a joint report on recommended projects, and Beck offered his own "policy report" to the president.

The joint report called for the federal government to purchase a variety of lands, including the following: 4 million acres for migratory waterfowl and shorebird breeding and nesting grounds; 2 million acres for the restoration of big game, fur bearers, and other mammals; 1 million acres of breeding and nesting areas for insectivorous, ornamental, and nongame birds; and 5 million acres of submarginal lands for upland game (this last amount was to be increased to 10 million acres contingent on the availability of suitable, unprofitable agricultural lands). The report also recommended allocating $25 million to start the refuge acquisition

Endangered light-footed clapper rail at high tide in coastal marsh at the Tijuana Slough NWR, California.

Fulvous whistling ducks, a rare
sighting at the Blackwater NWR,
Maryland.

program and another $25 million for the restora-
tion and improvement of the lands acquired.
Administration officials attacked the plans as too
far-reaching. President Roosevelt was conspicu-
ously silent, much to the consternation of the
committee and the press. They soon learned,
however, that the report had been found under a
pile of documents near the president's bed.
Apparently he hadn't even read it.

His work done, Darling returned to Iowa and
his cartooning. Then came a most unexpected
request. Would Darling, Roosevelt inquired,
return to Washington to head up the embattled
Bureau of Biological Survey? Darling's initial reaction was to say no. "A singed cat," Darling later
said, "was never more conscious of the dangers of
fire than I was of the hazards in trying to get anything done in Washington." And as a Republican
he was wary of appearing to "aid and abet" the
opposition. But this golden opportunity to promote wildlife protection and direct the organization that would take the lead in any duck recovery efforts was too good to turn down. He placed
his six-figure-income job as a political cartoonist
on hold and went back to Washington.

The thing that Darling and his beloved ducks
needed most was money. Within six days of
Darling taking over as head of the Bureau of
Biological Survey, a new mechanism for getting
that money materialized. On March 16, 1934,
Roosevelt signed the Migratory Bird Hunting
Stamp Act. Commonly referred to as the duck
stamp act, the new law required any person sixteen years or older hunting ducks, geese, swans,
or brant to have a $1 duck stamp and a valid
state hunting license. The stamps were distributed through U.S. post offices, and hunters were
required to affix them to their hunting licenses.
Revenues generated by the sale of duck stamps
were to be used primarily for the purchase,
maintenance, and development of "inviolate

President Franklin Delano
Roosevelt. *Library of Congress.*

RIGHT: Aldo Leopold studying a
bird specimen in 1942. "For us in
the minority," he wrote, "the
opportunity to see geese is more
important than television, and
the chance to find a pasque-
flower is a right as inalienable as
free speech." Leopold defined
game management as "the art of
making land produce sustained
annual crops of wildlife for
recreational use." *Library of
Congress.*

refuges." Fifteen years after the idea of a duck
stamp first appeared on the national scene, and
many legislative battles later, the stamp was
finally a reality.

The duck stamp act promised a healthy
stream of revenues, but it would not start for
at least a year. Darling did not want to wait
that long, especially since the ducks were in
such trouble. By one estimate 1934 marked an
all-time low for migratory waterfowl populations—twenty-seven million. And with every
passing month, more valuable waterfowl habitat would be plowed under, developed, or
dried up, and the prices of what remained
would continue to rise. Before Darling
accepted his new position, he asked Roosevelt
to reaffirm his $1 million pledge. The president
obliged and even invited Darling to "smoke a
good cigarette" to seal their deal. When
Darling came calling to collect, Roosevelt
wrote out an IOU for $1 million and told

Darling to use it to get money from some part
of the administration.

Darling thought the IOU, which he called a
chit, was money in the bank. "No small boy with
a new cowboy hat and Texas boots ever felt more
like a big shot than I did walking out of the White
House with my first . . . [chit] signed with the
familiar 'F.D.R.' in his own handwriting!" The
excitement soon faded as Darling was shunted
from one official to another, all of whom regarded
the chit with gravity and said, in effect, "sorry, just
don't have the money." As Darling's frustration
mounted, he began to wonder if he were caught in
a game of cat and mouse or, worse, that his travails
were all part of one of Roosevelt's famous practical
jokes. One interaction was particularly galling to
Darling. He had been hammering away at Harry
Hopkins, the head of the Works Progress
Administration, the Civil Works Administration,
and the Federal Emergency Relief Administration.
Hopkins controlled billions of dollars of aid.

Surely, Darling thought, he could spare a million. Hopkins finally agreed and told Darling to come back the next morning at nine sharp. Before leaving for the meeting that day, Darling read the newspaper and saw a startling headline, "Harry Hopkins Sails for Europe." The article said Hopkins had left the night before. Darling marched over to Hopkins's office and spoke to his assistant, who had no knowledge of the money and no interest in Darling's explanation of the promise his boss had made.

Instead of giving up, Darling changed venues and pursued the $1 million on Capitol Hill. He enlisted the support of Senator Peter Norbeck, the man who had led the charge for the passage of the Migratory Bird Conservation Act and the duck stamp act. Norbeck agreed to fight to get the Bureau of Biological Survey $1 million from

the last year's unexpended federal relief funds that it could use to purchase refuges. He got that and more in what Darling called "one of the funniest incidents of the whole restoration procedure." Norbeck had planned to add the request to a rider that would be attached to the omnibus bill for the survey. On the final day of debate over the bill, Norbeck asked Carl D. Shoemaker, secretary of the Special Senate Committee on Wildlife, to come by his office and draft the rider. But instead of asking for $1 million, Norbeck told Shoemaker to up the amount to $6 million. Then the two of them walked over to the Senate chamber. Along the way Norbeck, who had recently had all of his teeth pulled out, complained that his dentures were hurting, so he took them out and dropped them into his vest pocket. As Norbeck walked

"What a Few More Seasons Will Do to the Ducks" (September 17, 1930) by Ding Darling. *Courtesy of the J. N. "Ding" Darling Foundation.*

RIGHT: "Why Call Them Sportsmen?" (March 26, 1932) by Ding Darling. *Courtesy of the J. N. "Ding" Darling Foundation.*

Snow and blue geese feeding on the new growth following a prescribed burn at the Anahuac NWR, Texas. Most of this 34,000-acre refuge was paid for by federal duck stamp revenues.

onto the Senate floor, the omnibus bill was coming up for a vote. He rushed down the aisle and thrust the rider into the clerk's hand. The presiding senator, Champ Clark, directed the clerk to read it aloud, which he did, quickly and not very clearly. Clark then asked Norbeck to read the rider as well. Norbeck had a thick Scandinavian accent and was difficult to understand when he had his dentures in; with his dentures out he was almost incomprehensible. Shoemaker later recalled that Norbeck's words sounded like "glut, glut, oogle, glut." Still, even though it is doubtful that

members in the chamber knew what was in the rider, they passed it unanimously, most likely out of deep respect for their colleague who had fought so long on behalf of migratory waterfowl and who, they all knew, was fighting a losing battle against cancer. Norbeck then successfully steered the omnibus bill through the Senate-House conference committee, whereupon it was sent to the White House for the president's signature. Roosevelt was busy readying himself for a fishing trip in the Caribbean, and he signed the bill after giving it a cursory glance. When

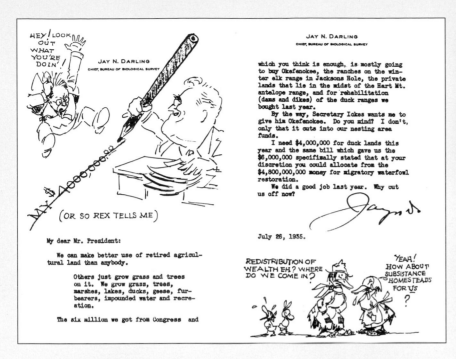

Roosevelt left for vacation the next morning, he was unaware that he had just given the Bureau of Biological Survey $6 million.

Soon after getting the $6 million, Darling sent Roosevelt an illustrated letter asking him to save $4 million in Bureau of Biological Survey funding that Darling had heard was going to be cut. Darling implored, "We can make better use of retired agricultural land than anybody. Others just grow grass and trees on it. We grow grass, trees, marshes, lakes, ducks, geese, furbearers, impounded water and recreation. . . . I need $4,000,000 for duck lands this year. . . . We did a good job last year. Why cut us off now?" Roosevelt replied, "As I was saying to the Acting Director of the Budget the other day—'this fellow Darling is the only man in history who got an appropriation through Congress, past the Budget [agency] and signed by the President without anybody realizing that the Treasury had been raided.' You hold an all-time record. . . . Nevertheless, more power to your arm! Go ahead with the six million . . . and talk to me about a month hence in regard to additional lands, *if* I have any more money left."

Ding Darling's illustrated letter urging Roosevelt to free up more money for the purchase and restoration of refuges. *Courtesy of the J. N. "Ding" Darling Foundation.*

RIGHT: To keep up with the rising costs of purchasing land and to expand the impact of the duck stamp program, duck stamp prices have gone up seven times, to the point where today a duck stamp costs $15.
Top: The first federal duck stamp, with an image of mallards alighting on a marsh. It was based on a drawing by Ding Darling titled "Mallards Dropping In."
Middle: The 1988 federal duck stamp, depicting Daniel Smith's painting of a snow goose.
Bottom: The 1999 federal duck stamp, depicting Jim Hautman's painting of greater scaup. Each year, in Washington, D.C., there is a major art competition to determine the image that will appear on the next year's duck stamp. This stamp represents the third time Jim Hautman has won the competition.
U.S. Fish and Wildlife Service.

9

THE GLORY YEARS

Darling's energy, enthusiasm, vision, and uncanny ability, as he said, to suck "funds for wildlife out of the other fellow's barrel" transformed the demoralized Bureau of Biological Survey into an organization brimming with confidence and renewed purpose. His reshuffle of personnel at the survey was followed, he said, "by the relief that comes from extracting a badly ulcerated tooth. The soreness did not last long, and the way the majority of the people in the bureau—like hungry bass—snapped at the lures of constructive work to be done, was an unexpected pleasure." This was especially true for the struggling refuge system, where Darling combined funding with truly outstanding staff selections to get things moving.

Darling's first step was to get someone to take the lead in refuge acquisition. Every day that passed, more acres of prime habitat were lost, and Darling well knew that the cost of the remaining acres was climbing. Darling immediately thought back to his days as a member of the Iowa State Conservation Commission and to one of his employees, John Clark Salyer II, an active, knowledgeable, redheaded wildlife biologist

Prescribed burn viewed from the air at the Florida Panther NWR, Florida.

95

Mallard hen at the Erie NWR, Pennsylvania.

BELOW: John Clark Salyer II. He retired as chief of refuge management in 1961. A year later, the Department of the Interior honored him with its Distinguished Service Award. *U.S. Fish and Wildlife Service.*

RIGHT: Golden eagle nest on cliff above the Green River at the Seekskadee NWR, Wyoming.

from Missouri with a deep love for the outdoors. When Darling became the survey's chief, Salyer was busy pursuing his Ph.D. in biology at the University of Michigan and was intent on becoming a professor. Darling called on Salyer in the spring of 1934 and implored him to come to Washington to oversee the management and growth of the refuge system. Salyer, realizing this was a once-in-a-lifetime opportunity, took a one-year leave from the University of Michigan and drove to the nation's capital in June. Fortunately for the refuge system and everyone who cares about it, Salyer never returned to finish his degree. On December 17, 1934, he accepted a permanent position, becoming chief of the Division of Migratory Waterfowl, and thirty years later he retired as chief of refuge management after an illustrious and productive career.

Salyer's first task was to quickly spend a big chunk of the money Darling had engineered, and fast. The survey had until March 31, 1935, to use $2.5 million in Works Progress Administration funding, whereupon any unexpended amount would go to other agencies. No sooner had Salyer settled in Washington than he was off, crisscrossing the countryside in a government-issued Oldsmobile. This mode of transportation was not selected for speed but because Salyer was reportedly deathly afraid of planes and trains. Spending the money was not as simple as writing a check. Land had to be identified and evaluated, improvements to refuges mapped out, land sales negotiated, and the transfers to the government approved by the secretary of agriculture. Of course, Salyer did not start from scratch. The Committee on Wild-Life Restoration provided many options, and the survey personnel for years had been identifying potential refuges in the hope that money would become available. Still, Salyer's task was Herculean, but that didn't phase him one bit.

Salyer pushed himself relentlessly. Apparently, his zeal was reflected in his driving, and over time more than a few survey staff refused to accompany him on the road. When he wasn't driving fast, he was gesticulating with his hands, often pointing out the window to this or that piece of prime habitat. One refuge manager, who once followed Salyer's car through a refuge, remarked: "Look at those arms waving. He's not even driving with his hands. And every time his hand goes out that window it means spending another thousand dollars we don't have." According to George Laycock, a great chronicler of the refuge system, "within six weeks [Salyer] . . . had driven eighteen thousand miles and drawn up plans for 600,000 acres of new refuge lands." And he kept going with ever more determination as the March 31 deadline approached.

On Friday, March 29, Salyer returned to his office. He and his staff had allocated all but $250,000 of the $2.5 million. They wanted to allocate that as well, but they had run out of time. And even the amount he had provisionally spent would amount to nothing if the paperwork was not completed and signed by Secretary of Agriculture Henry Wallace. So, according to Laycock's account, Salyer and his secretary worked late preparing the documents. The next morning Salyer faced a difficult decision. Wallace wouldn't be back until Monday morning, a day after the March 31 deadline. Salyer could either miss the deadline or sign the papers on the secretary's behalf. He signed. Salyer later remarked, "I could have gone to prison. That was the longest weekend I ever spent." On Monday morning Salyer walked into Wallace's office, confessed his misdeed, and steadied himself. "You came in here to buy land," said Wallace, "go on back to work."

Among the gems that were protected during

Trumpeter swans and Canada geese wintering at the Lacreek NWR, South Dakota.

RIGHT, ABOVE: Upper Red Rock Lake with Gravelly Range in distance at the Red Rock Lakes NWR, Montana.

RIGHT, BELOW: A rehabilitated endangered bald eagle used in the public education programs at the Rocky Mountain Arsenal NWR, Colorado.

this blizzard of activity was Red Rock Lakes Refuge in Montana, established by executive order in 1935 to save the largest species of native North American waterfowl, the trumpeter swan. This magnificent creature stands up to 4 feet tall, has wingspans approaching 7 feet, and can weigh 30 pounds. Trumpeters have a call that is loud, sonorous, and deep, like a bass horn. When early settlers first heard the big bird's call, the sound was, they thought, like that made by "trompeters," hence its name. To give readers a "perfect conception of the beauty and elegance" of these birds, Audubon wrote,

> You must observe them when they are not aware of your proximity, and as they glide over the waters of some secluded island pool. On such

occasions, the neck, which at other times is held stiffly upright, moves in graceful curves, now bent forward, now inclined backward over the body. Now with an extended scooping movement the head becomes immersed for a moment, and with a sudden effort a flood of water is thrown over the back and wings, when it is seen rolling off in sparkling globules, like so many large pearls. The bird then shakes its wings, beats the water, and as if giddy with delight shoots away, gliding over and beneath the liquid element with surprising agility and grace. Imagine . . . that a flock of fifty swans are thus sporting before you, as they have more than once in my sight, and you will feel, as I have felt, more happy and void of care than I can describe.

Once distributed widely throughout North America, the mighty trumpeter, prized for its brilliant snowy white plumage, was nearly hunted to extinction in the late 1800s. The Hudson's Bay

Company alone handled 17,671 swan skins between 1853 and 1877, the majority of which came from trumpeters. At the end of the century, some residents of the Red Rock Lakes region got into the business of collecting young trumpeters, called *cygnets,* and selling them to zoos and parks all over the world. A pair of cygnets could fetch $75, a princely sum at the time.

In 1912 an ornithologist opined that the trumpeter's "total extinction is now only a matter of years. Its trumpeting call will soon be locked in the silence of the past." But then in 1919 a couple of breeding pairs were found in Yellowstone National Park. In 1932 sixty-nine more trumpeters were found over the mountains from Yellowstone in the Centennial Valley. Yet the fate of the species still hung in the balance. It is not surprising, therefore, that when Darling and Salyer began searching for refuge lands, one of their first goals was to help the trumpeters survive. And the Red Rock Lakes NWR, a place where trumpeters find a safe haven, has certainly contributed to the comeback of this species. Today, there are roughly twenty-five thousand wild trumpeters in the lower forty-eight states and Alaska.

Salyer was known as much for his brilliance and dedication as his temper. According to Laycock, shortly after assuming the position as chief of the Division of Migratory Waterfowl, Salyer became incensed over the attorney general's failure to expeditiously sign the papers for buying the land that would allow for the creation of the White River Refuge. With every passing day Salyer became more concerned that the opportunity might slip away. "Those papers," Salyer recalled, "had been gathering dust there for three

months." When he had had enough, Salyer called the attorney general's office and demanded to speak to the man himself. Salyer said, "I just gave him particular hell." The attorney general then called Secretary Wallace and asked, "who is this new assistant you have over there in refuges?" Wallace then called Salyer. "I don't know how you did things out in Michigan," he said, "but here in Washington you don't bawl out the Attorney General of the United States."

Darling was not only interested in adding land to the refuge system. He also wanted to improve the management and protection of the land that the Bureau of Biological Survey already controlled. To that end he began the process of hiring college-trained refuge managers, some of whom had degrees in the relatively new field of wildlife management. Leopold and others had argued for years that wildlife conservation efforts could greatly benefit from a more scientific

approach, applied by a new cadre of wildlife professionals. This expertise was especially needed on refuge lands, most of which were in rough shape, having been ditched, drained, eroded, plowed under, or otherwise impaired. The new, highly trained refuge managers had the skills necessary to restore these submarginal lands to prime wildlife habitat and to create conditions conducive to wildlife conservation.

Darling also focused on the existing refuges in need of the most help. One of those was the relatively new Charles Sheldon National Antelope Refuge. Creating the refuge didn't impress or greatly affect the cattle ranchers and sheepherders in the area. They ran their animals over the refuge as they pleased. After all, the refuge had never been fenced off, and it had plenty of forage for livestock. Observing the devastation, Darling remarked that the refuge "was the most desolate piece of the American continent I had ever visited." It had been "so mistreated that even a grasshopper would starve to death. There weren't enough sage hens left to tempt a hungry coyote and the few hardy pronghorned antelope which remained on that area were approaching extinction and none of their progeny lived over the next winter after they were born." Darling found the money to fence off the refuge. Within a year's time ryegrass and bunchgrass had returned in profusion, enabling the formerly parched soil to retain water. Water holes, long since forgotten, returned. If people needed further proof that the fence made the difference, all they needed to do was look on the other side of it, outside the refuge, where grasses continued to be eaten down to the ground and the land was dry as brick.

In ill health Darling stepped down as the head of the Bureau of Biological Survey on November 15, 1935, to return to private life, cartooning, and a less hectic routine. "The jig is

© 1999 J.N. "Ding" Darling Foundation

up," he wrote in a letter to Salyer. "My engine got overheated and my valves began to leak. An examination in Rochester left me only one choice, to either get out or slow down on the job to a snail's pace. I tried the latter, but can't do it." In his valedictory speech, Darling offered great insight into the obstacles facing those who would side with wildlife.

I have come to realize that most of our wildlife conservation troubles are due to lack of organization among those who are interested but ineffective in the conservation of wildlife. There is no mass strength to enforce adequate legislative and executive attention to wildlife interests. Every other element of American life has a national

A blue-winged teal with young at the J. Clark Salyer NWR, North Dakota. This refuge was originally called the Lower Souris NWR but was renamed on September 20, 1967, in honor of the man who had not only overseen the establishment of the refuge in 1935 but who had also done so much for the refuge system during his long career. In 1956 Ding Darling said of him, "It is my earnestly considered judgement that no man in America, in my generation, has single-handedly and alone restored, created and dedicated as many thousands of acres of wildlife habitat as J. Clark Salyer."

organization to get effective results. Wildlife interests remind me of an unorganized army, beaten in every battle, zealous and brave but unable to combat the trained legions who are organized to get what they want.

Many thought that Salyer would succeed Darling as chief, but Darling instead recommended Ira Gabrielson, who got the job. Gabrielson had joined the survey in 1915 as an assistant in economic ornithology, and he was working for the survey in the northwestern United States when Darling assumed the mantle of chief. Darling first met Gabrielson during a meeting of ten field men from the Northwest held in Washington, D.C. As Darling recalled, "among them was a very large pachyderm type of man with decided bucolic attributes. . . . He didn't look like much but when his turn came to speak for his section of the country he immedi-

ately justified his position by a very well-stated analysis." Darling liked what he heard so much that he brought Gabrielson to Washington to be a consulting specialist.

In a letter to Salyer, Darling tried to lessen the blow of selecting Garbrielson to succeed him by explaining the rationale for his choice.

> I put your qualifications—all of them, which included the most powerful personality and the

most vigorous leadership and technical qualifications with one black mark against you, i.e. your ability to think of more caustic things to say than anyone in the world and saying them instead of keeping some of them to yourself—up to the Secretary and set over against them the qualifications of Gabrielson who has many of your traits with a muffler on his disposition.

Darling later recalled the importance of Salyer to the refuge system. "To me," Darling said, "Salyer

was the salvation of the duck restoration program of 1934–36. He could make a water analysis in the back end of his battered old automobile. He did most of the work for which I was awarded medals." Whatever disappointment Salyer might have felt with this turn of events, it had virtually no impact on his drive to grow the refuge system. Up to the start of World War II, he, along with Gabrielson and numerous other dedicated, hard-working refuge employees, plowed ahead, building on the foundation Darling had provided. It seemed as if every couple of weeks the survey would issue another press release announcing an addition or improvement to the refuge system.

In 1936 Roosevelt created the Desert Game Range, spanning over 2 million acres of dramatic Nevada Xeriscape northwest of Las Vegas. The intended beneficiaries of the range were desert

Mojave desert with mallow in bloom at the Desert NWR, Nevada, which is the largest refuge in the lower forty-eight. The U.S. Air Force has bombing rights to much of the refuge that have been exercised on many occasions, fueling a heated debate over the impact of such activities on wildlife.

bighorn sheep. The males of the species, or rams, are best known for their massive curly horns, which can weigh upward of 30 pounds, as much as a fifth of their body weight. During rutting season sexually energized rams will often slam into each other head down and at full speed, creating a loud crack that can be heard for up to a mile away. As painful as this behavior looks, researchers have observed the same two rams butting their heads forty or fifty times without any apparent ill effects. Beaten back by a changing climate, hunting, and diseases brought to the desert by domesticated sheep, the bighorns were at the time of the range's creation barely hanging on, literally and figuratively, to the cliffs and mountainsides of the desert southwest. In 1939 the embattled desert bighorn sheep got another helping hand with the creation of the Kofa and Cabeza Prieta Game Ranges, covering more than

1.5 million acres in southwestern Arizona. All three of these ranges have helped to increase the population of the desert bighorn. At Cabeza Prieta, for example, the population has risen from a low of fifty in 1939 to around five hundred today.

Also in 1936 the Patuxent Research Refuge was established by executive order in Belstville, Maryland, to provide the Bureau of Biological Survey with research necessary to better manage the refuge system. "There are many perplexing problems," noted the press release announcing the refuge's creation, "in the administration of wildlife in the eastern United States, as elsewhere. The investigations on the refuge should help solve them. These demonstration areas will serve as practical object lessons for landowners and others interested in wildlife restoration and management." At the dedication of the facilities on June 3, 1939, Secretary Wallace intoned, "This wildlife station, the first of its kind, is the manifestation of a national determination and a

national ability to conserve and administer wisely the organic resources and products of the soil—a priceless heritage to the generations of Americans yet to come." Over the years the Patuxent refuge has more than met the hopes that were outlined at its inception. Patuxent's research team was intimately involved in the early research on the adverse effects of pesticides on wildlife that helped hasten the banning or restriction of DDT and other dangerous pesticides in this country. Through its pioneering captive breeding and release projects, Patuxent has played a crucial role in the recovery of many endangered species, including the bald eagle, the whooping crane, and the California condor. The refuge has grown from an initial 2,670 acres to nearly 13,000, and it houses one of the largest visitor centers in the refuge system. In its 40,000 square feet of space, the center includes state-of-the-art exhibits on the value of wildlife research and endangered species recovery efforts.

Many of the refuges added in the late 1930s

LEFT: Beavertail prickly pear cactus in bloom at the Cabeza Prieta NWR, Arizona. This refuge is the size of Rhode Island and hugs 56 miles of the U.S.-Mexican border. It got its name, which is Spanish for "black-headed," from a granite mountain within its borders whose peak is covered with a layer of black lava.

MIDDLE: Desert bighorn at the Kofa NWR, Arizona.

BELOW: American bittern killing a snake at the Quivira NWR, Kansas. Quivira is the most centrally located refuge in the lower forty-eight and is a stopping-off point for nearly half of the shorebirds in the Central flyway as they migrate in the spring and fall.

Last light at the Rice Lake NWR, Minnesota. The refuge's name comes from Rice Lake, a 4,500-acre expanse of shallow water that supports large numbers of wildlife and a healthy crop of wild rice (the water is difficult to see because of the vegetation). Nutty in taste and chewy in texture, wild rice isn't a rice at all but a species of aquatic grass that can grow up to 10 feet tall. Wild rice was once a staple in the diet of Native Americans in the area. Today, the Chippewa Indians have exclusive rights to harvest wild rice at the refuge, and they do so each fall using the traditional method of tapping the grain into their pole-propelled canoes with ricing sticks.

chief of the Bureau of Biological Survey at the time, said, "Besides helping in the conservation of the Nation's resource in wild fowl, this unemployment-relief work will be of great educational value to the conservation corps workers and to the public. . . . They will gain an understanding and appreciation of the value of our national wild-life resources which they can share with their families and friends."

In 1936 5,600 men were working in twenty-eight refuges, all of them along one of the four flyways, the areas where the needs of migratory birds were greatest. Two years later, Gabrielson recognized the fifth anniversary of the CCC with a well-deserved appreciation.

> The CCC boys are making an invaluable contribution to the national wildlife restoration program. Five years ago when our wildlife resources, especially waterfowl, were in serious danger the Biological Survey had a restoration program. It lacked the means and man power to carry out that program. Then emergency funds for buying refuge areas became available and CCC help for developing them. The results being accomplished are laying the foundation for a wild life restoration program beyond our fondest dreams.

The Bureau of Biological Survey press release including Gabrielson's comments, then offered some of the impressive numbers generated by the "CCC boys" in 1937 alone: one million food-bearing trees and shrubs planted; 2 million cubic yards of earth built up to form water impoundment dikes; 1.5 million cubic yards of ditches and channels cleared; 250,000 board feet of lumber used to build water control structures; and approximately 300,000 cubic yards of rock and concrete to create dams. The press release also reflected on the value of the program in more personal terms.

> These CCC boys coming as they do from all walks of life, and all parts of the country have had an

opportunity to work with nature and watch how nature responds to those who work with it. City boys who never before saw ducks, geese, herons, egrets, sandhill cranes, pheasants and other wildlife have through the CCC had an opportunity to watch them through their mating and nesting. They have seen these miracles of nature and learned first-hand the lessons of conservation. We may well look to these bright-eyed lads for the fulfillment of our ideals. They are the America of tomorrow and are making our conservation history of today.

In the same year John N. Bruce, an engineer at the CCC camp on the Tamarac Refuge in Minnesota, gave voice to a connection with history that was likely shared by many of his peers. "Hence, we wake up and live again, in reality, those forgotten pioneer days of our forefathers, to bring back as near as possible, at least in this area, those same abundant conditions of nature as they existed before the advent of civilization."

In subsequent years the CCC work expanded, and at its height there were thirty-eight camps on refuges nationwide. By the time the program came to an end in 1942, fifty-three refuges had benefited from the work of CCC boys. In 1943 Gabrielson reflected on the program's impact, staring that "at first . . . [the creation of the CCC] did not seem of great interest to wildlife conservationists, but it was another of those happenings which none considered epochal at the time but which later have brought about startling results."

While the CCC camps were still in full swing, the refuge system got a new home. In 1939 the Bureau of Biological Survey was transferred from the Department of Agriculture to the Department of the Interior, and at the same time the Bureau of Fisheries was transferred from the Department of Commerce to the Interior. The two bureaus were then combined to create the U.S. Fish and Wildlife Service, and that is where the refuge sys-

tem has been housed to this day. Another less momentous change for the refuge system involved nomenclature. On August 1, 1940, President Roosevelt signed an executive order designating all refuges under the control of the Fish and Wildlife Service as national wildlife refuges (NWRs). A service press release explained the change.

> Previously Federal wildlife refuges had been identified variously as Reservations, Bird Reservations, Migratory Waterfowl Refuges, Migratory Bird Refuges, and Game and Wildlife Preserves. It was pointed out that though an area is sometimes established primarily for the benefit of a single species or of a group of animals, all wildlife is protected on the refuge. Thus "National Wildlife Refuge" is considered a more appropriate name.

The press release also noted that, despite this order, a small number of refuges would not change

Silver maple, cottonwood, and sycamore leaves floating at the Ohio River Islands NWR, located in West Virginia, Ohio, and Pennsylvania.

Osprey nesting at the
Mattamuskeet NWR, North
Carolina. The main feature of the
refuge is the 40,000-acre Lake
Mattamuskeet, the largest natural
lake in North Carolina.

RIGHT: Crested auklets on cliffs
at the Alaska Maritime NWR,
Alaska.

their titles, such as the National Bison Range and the Wichita Mountains Wildlife Refuge.

The advent of World War II brought many significant changes for the refuge system. A country focused on vanquishing foreign foes had to husband its financial resources and direct most of them to the war effort, which left less for other societal priorities, including wildlife conservation. New refuges were added, but the pace slowed. Still, the importance of wildlife was not forgotten. A full year before the bombing of Pearl Harbor catapulted the United States into the maelstrom of battle, Gabrielson noted that the "Conservation of wildlife is one way of making a country worth living in—a first essential in inspiring zealous defense." On April 25, 1942, at a sportsmen's banquet in the town of Wellsboro, Pennsylvania, there was a pledge card next to each plate that read, "I pledge my heart and my right hand to my flag and my country. I further pledge myself to help carry out the wildlife conservation programs, now in progress, to the end that your boy and my boy, now serving his country, may find good hunting and fishing he has a right to expect, when he returns to civil life."

More than preserving wildlife, many refuges directly supported the war effort. Thousands of acres of refuge lands were leased to private individuals for farming to provide food both here and for our troops overseas. In 1943 more than 4,645,000 acres of land on thirty-three refuges in eighteen states and the Alaskan Territory were being used by the army and navy for varied purposes, including bombing ranges, gunnery ranges, air bases, tank-maneuvering areas, and docking facilities for recreational activities of the troops in training.

While the country focused its energies on the war, the threats to wildlife remained. In October 1943 Gabrielson expressed growing concern for Alaskan wildlife, which he saw being negatively impacted by construction and population increases. "We hope to establish . . . [additional] refuges before important species of wildlife are destroyed rather than await that destruction and then go through the long, painful process of restoration that has been necessary in the states." Two years later, Gabrielson made a plea for more refuges, especially "duck hotels, places where hungry and tired ducks may come to rest without fear of being riddled by shot and where the table is always set with aquatic plants of the type preferred by waterfowl."

After the war the boys came home, and a huge number of them decided to go hunting, in part to get back to familiar patterns and establish a sense of normalcy. Shooting at ducks, geese, and other game was a welcome change from shooting at the enemy. In June 1946 nearly ten million hunting permits were issued, which was an all-time high to that point. In light of these new demographics, the importance of refuges became clearer. As Albert N. Day, Gabrielson's successor as director of the Fish and Wildlife Service, said, "Peace can be harder on wildlife than war."

As the country settled back into the rhythms of peacetime, Rachel Carson, then a relatively unknown information specialist at the Fish and Wildlife Service, proposed to her boss that the service publish a series of booklets to introduce the public to the refuge system and the need for wildlife conservation in general. Carson had been at the service since its creation and at the U.S. Bureau of Fisheries for a few years prior to that. She had long been a writer, both for the government and on her own as a freelancer. But the great fame that would be associated with her name was still years away when she came up with the idea for the refuge series. Soon after Day became the director of the Fish and Wildlife Service in early 1946, he approved Carson's idea for the Conservation in Action series. The Fish and Wildlife Service was especially excited about the series, viewing it as part of its larger efforts to encourage the public to visit and enjoy refuges.

Carson's first task was to select the refuges to profile, a list that ultimately included the Chincoteague NWR in Virginia; Parker River NWR in Massachusetts; Mattamuskeet NWR, Pea Island NWR, and Swanquarter NWR in North Carolina; Okefenokee NWR in Georgia; Bear River NWR in Utah; Red Rock Lakes NWR and National Bison Range in Montana; Aransas NWR in Texas; National Elk Refuge in Wyoming; and Charles Sheldon Antelope Range and Stillwater Wildlife Management Area in Nevada. With that done, she was off, and over the next year and a half, she traveled the country to gather materials and insights for the series.

Carson pursued her task with great excitement and energy, accompanied by colleague and friend Katherine Howe, who contributed illustrations and photographs to the

project. Carson, never shy about gathering information to make a strong case for conservation, took copious notes in the field as she and her companion tromped through the refuges, invariably one step behind the refuge managers who were doing their best to answer all of the questions posed by their guests. From Parker River, Carson wrote to her friend Shirley Briggs that her days there were "full of command cars, marshes, mud, sand dunes, mosquitoes, and Audubonites," a regimen that left them "sunburned, black-and-blue, mosquito-bitten and weary." During a four day visit to Mattamuskeet, Carson and Howe stayed in a lodge that had been converted from an old water-pumping station by the CCC. The lodge had a spiral staircase winding up the old smokestack that afforded them a breathtaking panoramic view of the refuge. One morning, Carson awoke before dawn to indulge her passion for birding. Along a canal she was treated to a performance that she later recounted in a letter to a friend. "We heard them [the whistling swans], too, various conversational notes and—really a thrill—the high, thin note, almost a woodwind quality, that presumably gives them their name. . . . I still think the sound of a large flock of geese is one of the most thrilling in the world." After her visits to the refuges and in gratitude for the hospitality offered, Carson would send her hosts an inscribed copy of her first book, *Under the Sea Wind*.

The Conservation in Action series was published between 1947 and 1957, but Carson was at the Fish and Wildlife Service for only half of that time. The publication of Carson's *The Sea around Us* in 1951, which remained on the *New York Times* best-seller list for eighty-one weeks, launched her onto the world literary scene and provided enough royalties for her to leave her position. On forms requesting that her resignation be made effective on June 3, 1952, Carson listed her reason for resigning as follows: "To

Salt marsh at the Rachel Carson NWR, Maine. This refuge, which is scattered over 45 miles along the coast, captures the rugged natural beauty of Maine that Carson loved so much. In 1946 after her first trip to Maine, Carson wrote to a friend that her greatest ambition was to buy a house in Maine "and then manage to spend a great deal of time in it summers at least!"

devote my time to writing." Carson followed *The Sea around Us* with another popular book on the marine world, titled *The Edge of the Sea*. But it was the publication of *Silent Spring* in 1962 that catapulted her from the ranks of noted literary writers to the status of being an important figure in American and world history. Her eloquent and damning critique of pesticides and their lethal effects on ecosystems sparked a global debate on humankind's use of chemicals in general and their impact on nature and humans. Unfortunately, her passionate and powerful voice was cut short in 1964 when she succumbed to cancer at the age of fifty-seven.

Carson's impact on the Conservation in Action series went well beyond selecting refuges and doing background research. She penned a simple and graceful introduction to the series.

> If you travel much in the wilder sections of our country, sooner or later you are likely to meet the sign of the flying goose—the emblem of the National Wildlife Refuges.
> You may meet it by the side of a road crossing miles of flat prairie in the middle West, or in the hot deserts of the Southwest. You may meet it by some mountain lake, or as you push your boat through the winding salty creeks of a coastal marsh.
> Wherever you meet this sign, respect it. It

means that the land behind the sign has been dedicated by the American people to preserving, for themselves and their children, as much of our native wildlife as can be retained along with our modern civilization.

Wild creatures, like men, must have a place to live. As civilization creates cities, builds highways, and drains marshes, it takes away, little by little, the land that is suitable for wildlife. And as their space for living dwindles, the wildlife populations themselves decline. Refuges resist this trend by saving some areas from encroachment, and preserving them, or restoring where necessary, the conditions that wild things need in order to live.

Carson also wrote the first four booklets in the series—covering the Chincoteague NWR, Parker River NWR, and Mattamuskeet NWR and including one introductory booklet titled *Guarding Our Natural Resources*—and she coauthored, with Vanez Wilson, the fifth on Bear River. In *Guarding Our Natural Resources,* she told "the story of the wildlife resources of America, of their place in our history, and their value in our modern life." In forty-six pages Carson painted a loving picture of why all citizens should care about wildlife and how the government had taken steps to ensure that wildlife would have a bright future. "We in the United States of America," she wrote, "have been slow to learn that our wildlife, like other forms of natural wealth, must be vigorously protected if we are to continue to enjoy its benefits. . . . We . . . have much to accomplish before we can feel assured of passing on to future generations a land as richly endowed in natural wealth as the one we live in."

Carson's writing, always informative and

often beautiful and moving, created lasting images in the reader's mind. Of the Parker River NWR she said,

> Lying to the west, almost like another vast green sea, are the salt meadows. The winding Plum Island River, the lower reaches of the Parker, and all their small, meandering tributaries traverse the marshes with an intricate series of open-water canals. . . . After the lull of midsummer, when only a few [black] ducks are to be found here, migrants are coming in from the north. . . . Today perhaps there are a thousand. Tomorrow morning there may be five thousand; next week as many more.

Of the Mattamuskeet NWR she wrote,

> The rhythmic softness of the Indian name recalls the days when tribes of the Algonquin roamed the flat plains of the coast and hunted game in deep forests of cypress and pine. The Indians are gone, leaving few traces upon the land they once knew. Much of the forest as the Indians knew it is gone, too, but even today some of the wildest country of the Atlantic Coast is to be found in this easternmost part of the Carolina mainland.

The few years Carson spent working on the Conservation in Action series were, according to Carson biographer Linda Lear, "her happiest and most fulfilling time in the service." The Fish and Wildlife Service honored its former employee in 1969 by naming a refuge after her along the southern coast of Maine, not too far from Carson's summer home, a retreat she deeply treasured. The Rachel Carson NWR, scattered over 45 miles of Maine's coastline, provides habitat for numerous species of waterfowl and shorebirds and serves as a fitting tribute to Carson's love for birds and the refuge system.

LEFT: Endangered salt marsh bird's-beak at the Tijuana Slough NWR, California.

MIDDLE: Rachel Carson testifying on pesticide use before the Senate Government Operations Subcommittee in 1963. Carson once said, "Those who contemplate the beauty of the earth find reserves of strength that will endure as long as life lasts." *Library of Congress.*

BELOW: Refuge boundary sign at the Kootenai NWR, Idaho. The flying blue goose on the sign is the logo for the refuge system and was originally designed by Ding Darling.

10

CONFLICT, CONTROVERSY, AND COMPROMISE

As Rachel Carson was coming to the end of her career at the U.S. Fish and Wildlife Service, the refuge system was entering a troubling period of increased stress and strain. For decades many refuges had supported a wide range of nonwildlife-oriented activities, including farming, mining, hunting, and oil and gas exploration. In many instances such uses were legally permissible and compatible with the wildlife purposes for which the refuges were established. For example, on some refuges private interests held the rights to minerals or petroleum resources. On other refuges selective hunting was used as a means of controlling animal populations that were overwhelming the carrying capacity of the land. However, some proposed and actual uses of refuges were inappropriate. One of the more infamous examples of this transpired on the eve of World War II. Conservationists were alarmed by the army's plan to use the Red Rock Lakes NWR as an artillery range, and they urged President Franklin Delano Roosevelt to intervene to protect the local population of trumpeter swans. Roosevelt with a memorandum to the secretary of war, ordering him to

Horned lizard at the Pixley NWR, California.

Trumpeter swans asleep in the mist at the National Elk Refuge, Wyoming.

scrap the plan. "The verdict is for the Trumpeter Swan," Roosevelt wrote, "and against the Army. The Army must find a different nesting place." During the late 1940s and the 1950s, an increasing number of conflicts arose over the proper use of refuge lands.

Not long after the end of World War II, developers focused their sights on exploiting shell deposits located beneath the surface of the Sabine NWR, which sits along the Gulf Coast of

Louisiana. John Clark Salyer II was amazed at this turn of events. "Lo and behold," he wrote, "there came an unholy trio of politicians and they said they wanted permission to excavate shell beds from beneath" the refuge. Sabine was a major wintering ground for ducks and geese along the Mississippi flyway, and the opposition to the development plan was intense. In 1950 the Department of the Interior ruled against the developers, stating that the plan was contrary to

the principles of waterfowl management and would not be in the public interest.

In 1955 the air force proposed to drop phosphorous bombs within half a mile of the Aransas NWR along the coast of Texas. When the bombs exploded, they would light up the night sky for hundreds of miles and unleash a deafening roar. The air force gave little thought to how such a spectacle might affect the endangered whooping cranes, not to mention the other wildlife that made Aransas its home. Conservationists thought about it and got angry. When the air force dropped similar bombs over the Salt Plains NWR in Oklahoma, the few hundred thousand waterfowl in residence immediately left, no doubt a bit shell-shocked. With so few whooping cranes left, it was unconscionable, argued many, to test these devices on the edge of the Aransas NWR. What if the birds left the relative safety of the refuge and didn't return? Congress was flooded with letters of outrage. Op-ed writers protested the plan. Canada, concerned because the cranes nested there, officially asked the U.S. government to test somewhere else. The air force was outgunned, and it left the whooping cranes in peace.

The following year, the "Battle of Wichita Mountains" commenced. No shots were fired, but by the end of the battle, conservationists had won and the army had been defeated. It started when the officers at Fort Sill Military Reservation in Oklahoma decided that they needed to expand the military base at the expense of the Wichita

Mountains Wildlife Refuge, which lay next door. Few political difficulties were foreseen when the bill that would effect the land transfer was introduced on Capitol Hill. The army, after all, only wanted 10,700 acres.

But news traveled fast, and when conservationists heard that one of the crown jewels of the refuge system, the first game range established by Theodore Roosevelt, was on the chopping block, they mobilized their own army and attacked. Before the hearings commenced, five hundred letters arguing against the transfer had made it to the House subcommittee that would be considering the bill. At the hearings Representative John D. Dingell Jr. from Michigan laid down the gauntlet. "I am going to fight this land grab to the last minute of the hearing and fight it on the floor as hard as I am able and you can not get six inches of this or any other refuge unless you show me a better case than you have this morning." Salyer added, with his characteristic bluntness, "We have de-occupied Japan, the Philippines, and much of Germany, but not the refuges." As for the army's motives, Salyer was disgusted. "Make no mistake about it, any land the Army takes over becomes a private hunting club for the higher echelons plus some civilians that play the Army game." Instead of 10,700 acres, all the army got was a 3,600-foot-wide buffer zone for target practice along the southern part of the refuge.

Refuges were also coveted for the oil and gas contained beneath some of them. Between 1942 and 1953 the Department of the Interior issued twenty-two oil and gas exploration permits on refuges. During the next three years sixty-four such permits were issued. Part of the dramatic increase was due to the policies of Secretary of the Interior Douglas McKay, who was appointed by President Dwight D. Eisenhower in 1953 and served until 1956. Dubbed "Generous Doug" by

River of Boulders at the Wichita
Mountains Wildlife Refuge,
Oklahoma.

BELOW: An endangered brown
pelican at the Cedar Keys NWR,
Florida.

RIGHT: Oil rig at the Lacassine
NWR, Louisiana.

columnist Drew Pearson, McKay, a former used-
car salesman, not only put out the welcome mat
for oil and gas interests but also diverted duck
stamp revenues away from purchasing refuge
lands and used them for other projects. Perhaps
McKay's biggest impact on the refuge system
was in the area of personnel. Many of the Fish
and Wildlife Service's most dedicated staff were
shunted aside in favor of political appointees,
long on connections and short on experience.
One of the first to go was Albert N. Day,

director of the Fish and Wildlife Service. This so incensed Carson that she fired off a letter of protest to the *Washington Post* that was published on April 22, 1953. She viewed the dismissal of Day and other competent former colleagues as the first step in a "raid upon our natural resources that is without parallel within the present century." And she feared that such moves would "return us to the dark ages of unrestrained exploitation and destruction." When the Associated Press asked her to expound further on the events taking place at the Interior, Carson added, "The action against Mr. Day is an ominous threat to the cause of conservation and strongly suggests that our national resources are to become political plums."

Some of the assaults on the refuge system during this time were simply ludicrous. Gardener's Pinnacle, an impressive testament to the tenacity of rock in the face of the elements, juts out of the waters that are part of the Hawaiian Islands NWR. One morning, without giving warning to or getting permission from the Fish and Wildlife Service, a navy demolition team scaled the pinnacle and placed wires and explosives around it. A few minutes after the team scampered back down and had cleared the area, an explosion turned the top third of the pinnacle into a mass of boulders and rock fragments that rained down into the water. The only reason offered for this surreptitious attack was that the navy wanted to create a flat spot to land helicopters. Never mind that there were plenty of other places outside of the refuge to do so.

In 1952 Clarence Cottam, the assistant director of the Fish and Wildlife Service and one of the very able people Darling had elevated during his tenure, submitted his administrative-use-only "Report of Encroachments

Fishing in a cypress swamp at the Choctaw NWR, Alabama.

MIDDLE: Reviewing waterfowl hunting regulations at the Sand Lake NWR, South Dakota. *John and Karen Hollingsworth and the U.S. Fish and Wildlife Service.*

RIGHT: Northern cardinal at the Trustom Pond NWR, Rhode Island.

on National Wildlife Refuges," which offered a snapshot of current problems. After noting that "refuges are managed on a multiple-use basis" and that "grazing, farming, timber-cutting, haying, and trapping are encouraged" on many refuges, Cottam argued that in many instances the use and abuse of refuges had gone too far. The major culprits were military use and oil and gas drilling, but he also elaborated upon the threats posed by road, drainage, pipeline, and electrical transmission line right-of-ways, as well as water diversion, mining, lumbering operations, and even the efforts of powerful local interest groups to abolish entire refuges and convert them to some other use.

One of the most serious emerging pressures on the refuge system came from the people who used the refuges for recreation. In 1951, the first year records were kept, roughly three and a half million people visited refuges to hike, picnic, bird watch, hunt, and fish. By the end of the decade, visits exceeded ten million per year. While the Fish and Wildlife Service strongly encouraged people to visit refuges, the increased visitation meant increased impact on the land and wildlife. Some even began worrying that the refuges were in danger of being loved to death.

One group whose visitation was growing fast was hunters. Up through the late 1940s, many refuges had been off-limits to hunting. As originally envisioned, such refuges were supposed to aid the hunter by enabling protected bird populations to breed more freely, thereby producing greater numbers of birds for the hunters to pursue. This theory worked in practice, and oftentimes the best hunting was in areas adjoining refuges where hunting was not allowed. But by the end of the 1940s, many hunters were agitating for access to more of the refuges that their duck stamp dollars had helped to buy. Congress couldn't ignore these concerns, so it cut a deal. If more refuges were opened to hunting, the powerful hunting lobby agreed not to oppose Congress's desire to increase the price of the duck stamp from $1 to $2 so that additional money could be raised to purchase increasingly expensive refuge lands. With the bargain struck, Congress amended the duck stamp act in 1949, doubling the stamp's price while

allowing up to 25 percent of refuge lands purchased after 1949 with duck stamp money to be set aside for hunting. In 1958 another set of amendments raised the price of the stamp to $3 and the percentage of refuge land that might be opened to hunting to 40 percent. Then in 1966 another statutory change allowed for hunting on any refuge as long as such activity was determined to be compatible with the purposes for which the refuge was established.

There is hardly a more polarizing issue in the management of the refuge system than whether or not to permit hunting. The passions aroused during the 1920s debate over "public shooting grounds" were still easily fanned and have remained so right up until the present time. For some, responsible hunting is an oxymoron, and hunting itself is barbaric and should be banned

outright, not just on refuges. For others, hunting should be allowed, just not on refuges. Others still view hunting as a noble sport that should not only be allowed but also encouraged inside as well as outside of refuges. And those in favor of hunting on refuges can rightly point to the important role that hunters have played in the history of the refuge system. Regardless of where one stands on the issue of hunting, clearly opening more refuges to hunting further stressed the management capabilities of the refuge system.

Despite the turmoil of the 1950s, there were some bright spots. The 1958 amendments to the duck stamp act gave the government more money to purchase refuges. Up to that point many hunters thought that their duck stamp dollars were used solely to purchase land, but this was not the case. Since the inception of the duck stamp program, only 10 percent of the stamp revenues had gone to land acquisition; the remaining 90 percent had funded a wide range of activities, including refuge operations and maintenance, law enforcement, and research. The amendments increased the amount going toward land purchase to 100 percent minus printing costs. In practice that meant that roughly $.98 out of every dollar spent on duck stamps would, from then on, be used to acquire critical habitat. While this was good news for the physical expansion of the refuge system, it took resources away from operations and maintenance, functions that were already hurting due to years of chronically low funding.

The 1958 amendments also authorized the use of duck stamp funds to acquire small wetland potholes for use as waterfowl protection areas (WPAs). These lands, which average 223 acres, are located primarily in Nebraska, Montana, North and South Dakota, and Minnesota. Michigan has two, and Idaho and Maine each have one. Initially established on their own, WPAs were made part of the refuge system in 1966.

At first glance WPAs are not very impressive. Some are no more than small depressions in the prairie that are alternately wet and dry, filling with rainwater or melted snow, only to revert to cracked mud during hot or parched conditions. Others are wet year-round. In this case, however, appearances deceive. The thousands of WPAs, dubbed "duck factories," provide a critical lifeline to the rafts of migratory waterfowl that travel through the region by offering them places to rest, feed, and breed. Wetland management districts manage WPAs. One of the most important of these is the Rainwater Basin Wetland Management District in Nebraska.

Rainwater spans seventeen counties in south central Nebraska and oversees sixty-two WPAs encompassing nearly 24,000 acres. One of Rainwater's goals is to ensure the vigor of the mixed-species prairie upland grasslands it manages. This is done through a regimen of prescribed burning, grazing, haying, and harrowing of the land. When weeds such as Canada thistle and purple loosestrife invade the area, they are forcibly removed by mechanical, chemical, and biological treatments. Rainwater's staff also focuses on wetlands management, with the primary goal being to provide early successional wetlands rich in diverse annual plants on which migratory birds can feed. Although uplands and wetlands are managed in similar ways, wetlands require more frequent

LEFT: **Canada goose using manmade nesting structure at the Kootenai NWR, Idaho.**

Duck stamps are not just for hunters. Anyone who buys them contributes to the growth of the refuge system. It is one of the best investments in conservation an individual can make. Better yet, at those refuges that charge an entrance fee, a current federal duck stamp will get the bearer in free. *U.S. Fish and Wildlife Service.*

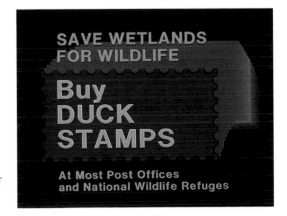

PRECEDING PAGES: Mallards at one of the WPAs managed by the Rainwater Basin Wetland Management District, Nebraska. WPAs have been referred to as the prairie jewels of the refuge system.

Endangered Key deer in a housing development and *(right)* at sunrise in the National Key Deer Refuge, Florida.

treatments to prevent single-species stands of late successional vegetation from dominating the area and thereby reducing the amount of food for waterfowl. The staff at Rainwater also works hard to minimize the outbreaks of avian cholera, a disease that killed as many as 120,000 birds in 1997. The disease is carried by snow geese and spread both bird to bird and water to bird. These forms of transmission make it especially important for there to be plenty of suitable habitat to avoid overcrowding that can trigger an outbreak. To that end Rainwater annually adds to the natural expanse of habitat by pumping water into some of its wetlands. Rainwater's efforts to provide suitable habitat for migratory waterfowl have been very successful. During the spring migration alone, the Rainwater Basin serves as a temporary home for roughly two to three million geese and seven to nine million ducks on their journey to the northern nesting grounds.

During the 1950s the refuge system added twenty-four refuges. One of the additions was the National Key Deer Refuge, established by Congress in 1957 and located 30 miles east of Key West in Florida. Its primary purpose is to protect the Key deer, a miniature version of its northern, white-tailed cousin. Key deer are sometimes referred to as "toy deer" for their diminutive stature. Standing between 24 and 32 inches at the shoulders, and weighing between 65 and 85 pounds, the Key deer is unique to Florida's lower keys, and by 1950 it was just barely hanging on. One estimate placed the deer's numbers between twenty-five and fifty. At the time two other NWRs were in the area, Key West and Great White Heron, but neither encompassed the habitat critical to the Key deer. And the state law prohibiting the hunting of the deer had little effect for lack of enforcement.

Things started changing in 1951, when the cash-strapped Fish and Wildlife Service, using

funds supplied first by the Boone and Crockett Club and then by the National Wildlife Federation, hired a big, burly, cigar-smoking, and, most of all, dedicated game warden by the name of Jack Watson to patrol the area. In short order, deer poaching dropped off, but Watson was only one man and he had a lot of ground to cover. Local pressure to protect the still-endangered Key deer percolated up through the political system and led to the creation of the refuge and the official appointment of Watson as its first manager. Land acquisition for the refuge was kicked off by a 15.5-acre donation to the Fish and Wildlife Service by the North American Wildlife Foundation. In subsequent years additional donations, purchases, and leasing arrangements have increased the size of the refuge to more than 9,000 acres, land that supports a herd of six hundred to eight hundred deer.

Although the Key deer population is increasing at 1–3 percent annually, it still faces serious threats. Fifty percent of the known Key deer deaths are due to highway accidents, and a significant number are the result of dog attacks, entanglements, drowning, and disease. Occasionally, the deer are illegally killed. In March 2000 a local resident found a decapitated Key deer during a walk through the refuge. It was determined to be a deliberate act and, as such, can be subject to a fine of up to $25,000 and one-year imprisonment under the authority of the Endangered Species Act. Although the perpetrator of this crime has not been caught, nearly ten years earlier a person who was caught and found guilty of killing a deer was sentenced to a year in prison; an accomplice received ten months.

11

NEW ROLES AND RESPONSIBILITIES

During the 1960s and 1970s, the United States experienced an environmental awakening. This transformation was spurred on by the publication of books such as *Silent Spring*, the outreach and advocacy work of a great variety of environmental and conservation groups, and the press's extensive coverage of stories exposing the widespread negative impacts of human activity on the environment. The public's increasing concern propelled its elected leaders to enact bold laws aimed at ameliorating many environmental problems. Much of the legislation focused on air, water, and land pollution. This was the era of the Clean Air Act, the Clean Water Act, and the Resource Conservation and Recovery Act, the last of which sought to improve the management and disposal of hazardous and nonhazardous wastes. It was also an era in which legislators sought to better protect the public's lands and the wildlife that depended on them. In

Sunrise over Ringneck Marsh at the Iroquois NWR, New York.

particular, the 1960s and 1970s were a time when many legislative changes affected the roles and responsibilities of the refuge system.

Canoeing through the Bond Swamp NWR, Georgia.

MIDDLE: Placing boundary signs for refuge wilderness area at the Agassiz NWR, Minnesota. According to Aldo Leopold, "Wilderness is the raw material out of which man has hammered the artifact called civilization."

RIGHT: Short-eared owl at dawn at the Lacreek NWR, South Dakota.

Congress passed the Refuge Recreation Act in 1962 to address the growing issue of public use. At some of the more popular refuges, refuge staffs were overwhelmed with the demands of handling hundreds of thousands of annual visitors, often concentrated on weekends. The staffs not only were hard-pressed to clean up after the deluge of people but also often had limited authority to regulate recreational activities. The Refuge Recreation Act was intended to improve this situation by providing a funding source to administer recreational activities and allowing such activities only when they didn't interfere with the purposes for which the refuge was established.

Two years later, in 1964, Congress created the Land and Water Conservation Fund, a source of money for the acquisition of federal lands including not only refuges but also national and state parks, forests, and other reserved areas. Congress directed that the money come primarily from fees paid by companies drilling for offshore oil and

gas, as well as from revenues generated by a motorboat fuel tax, user fees for recreational areas, and direct congressional appropriations. Since its inception the Land and Water Conservation Fund has funneled more than $1 billion to the Fish and Wildlife Service for the purchase of refuge lands.

The Wilderness Act, also passed in 1964, singled out for protection those federal lands "where the earth and its community of life are untrammeled by man, where man himself is a visitor who does not remain" and ordered that they be managed to ensure "the preservation of their wilderness character." Wilderness has long captured the imagination of Americans. Untamed lands have been viewed sometimes with fear but usually with love and respect. Margaret Murie, fondly called the grandmother of the conservation movement and the recipient of the Presidential Medal of Freedom for her life's work, said, "Wilderness itself is the basis of all our civilization. I wonder if we have enough reverence for life to concede to wilderness the right to live on?" And famed western writer Wallace Stegner argued that "Something will have gone out of us as a people if we ever let the remaining wilderness be destroyed. . . . We need wilderness preserved . . . because it was the challenge against which our character as a people was formed." Many imbue wilderness with an almost mystical ability to cleanse the body and the mind and, in doing so, sustain them. According to John Muir, "In God's wilderness lies the hope of the world—the great fresh, unblighted, unredeemed wilderness. The galling harness of civilization drops off, and the wounds heal ere we are aware." The same development and expansionary pressures that decimated wildlife populations throughout much of the history of the United States also eliminated vast areas of wilderness. The Wilderness Act reflected society's conclusion that the continued loss of wilderness would diminish society as well and if it didn't save these lands they would be lost forever. As Leopold said, "Wilderness is a resource which can shrink but not grow . . . the creation of new wilderness in the full sense of the word is impossible."

This concept of protecting areas in which human impact is minimal was not new to the refuge system. For many decades there had been refuges that by virtue of their remoteness and their character could easily qualify as wilderness. The new act gave the refuge system an opportunity to prove and expand upon this point. The Department of the Interior was one of the federal land agencies that the act directed to inventory its holdings and come back to Congress with recommendations for areas that should be designated as wilderness.

The inventorying process and subsequent designations and set-asides by Congress created nearly 21 million acres of wilderness on sixty-

four refuges. Over 90 percent of those acres are in Alaska; the remaining acres are spread throughout twenty-four of the lower forty-eight states. In 1968 about half of the Great Swamp NWR in New Jersey became the first part of the refuge system to be designated wilderness. Amazingly, this refuge is located a mere 26 miles west of New York City's Times Square and 7 miles south of Morristown, New Jersey, which dispels the notion that wilderness can only be found in places that are far away from civilization. The smallest wilderness area in the refuge system is the 2-acre Wisconsin Islands Wilderness, part of the Green Bay NWR. At the opposite extreme is the Arctic NWR, which contains 8 million acres of wilderness. Far from being out-of-bounds to humans, the refuge system's wilderness areas may be opened to a range of activities, including hunting, fishing, backpacking, education programs, research, and grazing, as long as such activities support approved refuge management goals.

In 1966, Congress passed the National Wildlife Refuge Administration Act, which

LEFT: Gray seals on a beach at the Monomoy NWR, Massachusetts. Ninety-seven percent of Monomoy is designated wilderness. The refuge is also the largest haul-out site for gray seals on the Atlantic seaboard.

Surf fishing at sunrise at the Hobe Sound NWR, Florida. The name of this refuge comes from a shipwreck in 1696. Survivors of the shipwrecked *Reformation* were captured and then given assistance by the Jobe (Hobe) Indians.

officially created the National Wildlife Refuge System by formally bringing the various units (such as refuges, game ranges, and WPAs) under one administrative umbrella. The act also, for the first time in history, attempted to provide general statutorily based management guidelines, the most important of which authorized the secretary of the interior to "permit the use of any area within the [Refuge] System for any purpose, including but not limited to hunting, fishing, public recreation and accommodations, and access whenever he determines that such uses are compatible with the major purposes for which such areas were established." This meant that refuge lands were not "single-use" lands but "dominant-use" lands, where primacy was accorded to the use for which the refuge was established yet other, secondary uses could also be allowed. Of course, refuges had long been used for varied purposes. The National Wildlife Refuge Administration Act just made the policy more explicit.

TOP: Measuring loggerhead turtle at the Archie Carr NWR, Florida. Archie Carr provides nesting habitat for roughly nineteen thousand threatened loggerheads, three thousand endangered green turtles, and about a dozen endangered leatherback turtles.

Endangered ocelot with radio collar at the Laguna Atascosa

NWR, Texas. The collars monitor the ocelots' travels so that a database can be built on the life histories of these rare creatures. The Friends of Laguna Atascosa sponsor an adopt-an-ocelot program that raises money for habitat protection and continuing research intended to aid this beautiful animal.

In 1968 the Wild and Scenic Rivers Act afforded the refuge system another opportunity to protect special places. The act declared it to be national policy that "certain selected rivers of the Nation, which, with their immediate environments, possess outstandingly remarkable scenic, recreational, geologic, fish and wildlife, historic, cultural or other similar values, shall be preserved in free-flowing condition, and that they and their immediate environments shall be protected for the benefit and enjoyment of present and future generations." Roughly 1,400 miles of wild and scenic rivers have been protected on five refuges in Alaska and along a portion of the Niobrara River on the Fort Niobrara NWR in Nebraska.

In 1973 President Richard M. Nixon signed the Endangered Species Act. He stated that "Nothing is more priceless or more worthy of preservation than the rich array of animal life with which our country has been blessed." The act has provided a lifeline to endangered animals and plants that are teetering on the edge of existence, whose numbers are so low that extinction is not unthinkable but imminent. The act has safeguarded threatened species as well—ones not currently in danger of extinction but which might become so in the foreseeable future. In addition to protecting individual species through legal restrictions on killing, harassing, possessing, and selling them, the act has also protected the critical habitat that those species need to survive, and this is one of the instances where the refuge system plays an important role.

The act gave the Fish and Wildlife Service the authority to purchase habitat for the protection of threatened and endangered species. Although the act formalized the relationship between the refuge system and endangered species, that relationship goes back to the early 1900s when pelicans,

MIDDLE: An endangered Delmarva fox squirrel at the Blackwater NWR, Maryland.

BELOW: Hawaiian black-necked stilts at the Hanalei NWR, Kauai, Hawaii, one of the many species of Hawaiian birds on the endangered list.

An endangered red wolf in the reintroduction program at the Alligator River NWR, North Carolina.

often called *seacows,* the manatee's closest relations are elephants, and there is clearly a family resemblance. Grayish, with wrinkled skin and a peaceful visage and demeanor, manatees average 10 feet long and can grow to over 1,000 pounds. They are generally slow-moving animals that feed exclusively on aquatic plants and can live for up to sixty years in captivity, but probably not quite that long in the wild. Requiring warm waters, above 68°F, manatees congregate in Florida during the winters, but in the summers they can venture as far north as Rhode Island and west to Texas. The refuge, which includes several small islands and water bottoms in Kings Bay at the headwaters of the Crystal River, is ideal for the manatees. More than thirty freshwater springs supply the area year-round with

600 million gallons daily at a constant 72°F. Of the 3,500 West Indian manatees in Florida, roughly 10 percent rely on the Crystal River NWR for critical habitat.

Spanish colonists in the 1500s were the first to exploit the completely defenseless manatees, killing them for their meat, oil, and skin, which was used to make leather. By the late nineteenth century, manatee populations were already dangerously low. In 1893, Florida banned manatee hunting, but subsequent habitat loss contributed to the continued decline of the species and led to its placement on the endangered species list. The Nature Conservancy, in concert with local citizens, raised money and purchased the refuge islands, which were subsequently bought by the Fish and Wildlife Service and brought into the refuge system. In addition to manatees the refuge is home to a variety of wildlife, including ospreys, egrets, herons, cormorants, alligators, gars, tarpon, and mullet.

The area surrounding the refuge is highly developed, and the manatees still face threats, the most pervasive of which are boating accidents. The manatees can be difficult for boaters to see, and the animals are often not capable of taking quick, evasive action to get out of harm's way. The scars left on manatees by propeller blades are sometimes so distinctive that researchers use them to identify specific individuals. In some cases the collisions are fatal. In 2001, of the 325 manatees that died in Florida waters, 81 of them succumbed to watercraft-related injuries. To minimize such dangers, the refuge has established idle and slow speed zones throughout Kings Bay, and when manatee concentrations are highest, manatee sanctuary areas are designated to provide the animals with places where they can feed and rest undisturbed. These efforts have succeeded in keeping the mortality rates low for manatees in and around the refuge.

The refuge system has not only created refuges specifically for endangered species but has also designated land in existing refuges to help such species survive. The red wolf provides an excellent example of this. Plentiful in the mid-Atlantic and southeastern United States when the colonists arrived, red wolves were soon undeservedly labeled as varmints and a threat to farmers and domestic livestock. Bounties and eradication programs followed, which combined with habitat loss and crossbreeding with coyotes to level the population. By the middle of the twentieth century, the red wolf was nearly an apparition. In 1970 there were fewer than one hundred red wolves hanging on in a small area of coastal Louisiana and Texas. To save the red wolves from extinction, the Fish and Wildlife Service, between

1974 and 1980, captured as many of the wild animals as it could. Fourteen of the most genetically pure became the nucleus of a captive-breeding program at the Point Defiance Zoo and Aquarium in Tacoma, Washington. Today, thirty-three zoos and nature centers nationwide participate in the breeding program.

In 1977 the Fish and Wildlife Service transferred a pair of captured red wolves to the Cape Romain NWR on Bulls Island off the coast of North Carolina. The goal was to see how the animals would do in a part of their historic range where they hadn't been seen for many years. After a brief period in acclimation pens, the pair was set loose. The male and female promptly swam to the next island, where the female was scared by dogs and swam to the mainland. She was captured and brought back to Bulls Island but soon died of a urinary tract infection. The male was sent to Tacoma, and Bulls Island received another pair of wolves. After only a short while, however, the Fish and Wildlife Service decided that the second pair was needed to bolster the gene pool of the captive breeding population, and they were also sent to Tacoma.

In 1987 the Alligator River NWR on the coast of North Carolina became the first place where red wolves from the captive-breeding program were reintroduced to the wild when a pair was released in the refuge. Shortly thereafter, another pair was sent to Bulls Island. Since their reintroduction the red wolves have begun clawing their way back to sustainability. In 1988 a litter of red wolf pups was born in the wild on the Alligator River NWR. The pair on Bulls Island has produced pups as well, and when they reach fifteen to twenty months old, they are sent up the coast to the Alligator River NWR. Today, there are about one hundred red wolves that range over 1.5 million acres that include not only the Alligator River NWR but also the Pocosin Lakes

and Mattamuskeet NWRs, as well as an air force and navy bombing range and private lands.

Whooping cranes provide one of the most fascinating stories of endangered species helped by the refuge system. They are the tallest birds in North America, peaking at 5 feet, most of that being taken up by their long necks and spindly legs. Juveniles are rusty brown, and adults have black legs and feet, red and black heads, long and pointed beaks, and snow-white body feathers with jet-black wingtips that are only visible during flight. Whooping cranes are named for their unusual call, which can be heard up to 2 miles and is generated by resonance in the bird's 5-foot-long trachea, half of which is coiled behind the breastbone. Whooping cranes mate for life and engage in a dramatic courtship dance consisting of calling, wing flapping, head bowing, and jumping high into the air. In flight whooping cranes are equally dramatic, using their 7-foot wingspan to power slow, methodical beats as they move across the sky, often flying at heights so great that they are invisible from the ground.

Whooping cranes were never plentiful. It is estimated that there might have been 15,000 of the birds in North America when the first Europeans arrived. Biologists believe that by 1865 the number had dwindled to between 700 and 1,400. Whooping cranes continued to suffer from the destruction of wetlands as well as hunting, the latter of which killed as many as 250 birds between 1870 and 1924. By the mid-1930s only two flocks of whooping cranes remained: a nonmigratory flock in coastal Louisiana and a migratory flock that nested in Wood Buffalo National Park in the Northwest Territories of Canada and wintered on the Blackjack Peninsula on the east coast of Texas. Concerned about the fate of these magnificent birds, and urged to action by the National Audubon Society and others, the Bureau of Biological Survey established the Aransas NWR in 1937 along the Texas Gulf coast to protect the last migratory flock.

It was almost too late. At the time both flocks of whooping cranes were on their last legs, literally and figuratively, with only a few dozen remaining. By the early 1940s the whooping crane population at the Aransas NWR had dropped to thirteen adults and two juveniles, and the Louisiana flock, which had been devastated by a hurricane in 1940, had only six birds left. In 1950 the lone survivor of the Louisiana flock, Mac, was captured and transferred to the Aransas NWR, where she soon died. Fortunately for the cranes this low point was the beginning of a long flight of recovery.

The protected Aransas NWR–Wood Buffalo National Park population grew slowly over time. Then in 1975 U.S. Fish and Wildlife Service and Canadian Wildlife Service biologists attempted to create a new migratory flock by placing whooping crane eggs in sandhill crane nests at the Grays Lake NWR in Idaho. The eggs were taken one at a time from clutches of two laid by wild whooping cranes at Wood Buffalo National Park, a move that didn't affect the viability of the flock because usually only a single chick survives. The idea was to have the sandhills, which are closely related to the whooping cranes but smaller and more numerous, act as foster parents for their cousins and then teach them to migrate from the Grays Lake NWR to the Bosque del Apache NWR in New Mexico, a much shorter distance than between Wood Buffalo National Park and the Aransas NWR. For a while the experiment seemed to work. The eggs hatched, and the sandhill parents taught their whooping crane wards to fend for themselves and migrate to and from Bosque del Apache NWR. But many of the whooping cranes were killed in collisions with power lines, while others succumbed to disease, predation by eagles, and hunters. The

biggest obstacle to the survival of the foster flock involved sex, or more precisely the lack of it. When the whooping cranes reached mating age, they had an "identity crisis" and became confused, attempting to mate with the sandhills and not their own kind; the net result—a single whooping crane/sandhill hybrid, otherwise known as a whoophill. Ultimately, the Grays Lake NWR whooping cranes disappeared.

Although the Grays Lake venture failed, captive-breeding programs have succeeded. In 1975 the Patuxent NWR in Maryland became the first captive-breeding site to close the reproductive loop when one of its whooping cranes laid eggs. Since that time other captive-breeding

Captive endangered whooping crane at the Patuxent Wildlife Research Center, Maryland.

BELOW: *(Left to right)* Hybrid whoophill with male whooping crane and female sandhill crane in November 1989 at the Bosque del Apache NWR, New Mexico.

Operation Migration pilot Deke Clark uses a puppet to teach whooping cranes to forage at an isolated stopover site in Wisconsin while waiting for the ground crew to prepare the temporary travel pen. Established in 1994, Operation Migration is a nonprofit organization in both Canada and the United States dedicated to the restoration of migration routes for endangered or threatened species of birds.

Operation Migration used ultralight aircraft and costume-isolation rearing techniques to teach a new and safe migratory pathway to whooping cranes. The organization's goal is to safeguard these magnificent birds from extinction by working as part of the Whooping Crane Eastern Partnership to establish a self-sustaining, migratory flock in eastern North America. *www.operationmigration.org.*

programs have had similar success, and the number of captive whooping cranes continues to grow. The ultimate goal of these programs is not to increase captive populations but to reestablish natural ones. This was especially important because there was always the possibility that a major disaster, such as a hurricane or an oil spill, could in an instant wipe out most of the wild whooping cranes. The governments of the United States and Canada, along with a range of private organizations, have been working in concert for many years to reintroduce captive whooping cranes into the wild. Beginning in 1993, captive whooping cranes were released in south-central Florida's Kissimmee Prairie, and today that nonmigratory population numbers around seventy-five.

In the late 1990s the Canadian and American International Whooping Crane Recovery Team recommended the establishment of a migratory whooping crane population in the eastern

United States, where wild populations of the birds hadn't been seen for one hundred years. To achieve this goal, the Whooping Crane Eastern Partnership, a consortium of nonprofits and government agencies, was created in 1998. The International Whooping Crane Recovery Team chose the Necedah NWR in Wisconsin as the location for the establishment of a new flock because it is within the historic range of the species and is far enough from the existing migratory flock so that the two won't interfere with each other. The plan was to have the new flock migrate from the Necedah NWR to the Chassahowitzka NWR in Florida. The big question was how do you teach newborn whooping cranes from Wisconsin to migrate to Florida come the fall? Enter an ultralight aircraft and the natural magic of imprinting.

The basic idea was that if newborn whooping cranes could be made to view the ultralight and the human handlers as surrogate parents, the cranes would follow the surrogates wherever they went. Before doing this with whooping cranes, the Whooping Crane Eastern Partnership tested the process with sandhill cranes. In May 2000, sandhill crane eggs were shipped to Patuxent Wildlife Research Center (within the Patuxent NWR and part of the U.S. Geological Survey). During incubation the eggs were exposed to the sounds of an ultralight, starting the imprinting process early. At less than two weeks old, the sandhills began exercising every day by following the ultralight. On June 30 the juveniles were flown to the Necedah NWR for more training.

During the sandhill cranes' stay at Patuxent Wildlife Research Center and the Necedah NWR, human contact was kept to a minimum. Handlers, who remained silent, were dressed head to toe in white fabric costumes and held sandhill crane head puppets in their hands in an effort to make them look like cranes. This was essential to the imprinting process and for ensuring that the birds did not become familiar with humans and, therefore, retain their natural skittishness around people. By October 3 the birds had mastered the skill of flying low and behind the ultralight, and more importantly, they appeared to view the ultralight and the handlers as surrogate parents. That day, the ultralight, its pilot, and eleven sandhills started migrating to the Chassahowitzka NWR, and many stops and a little over a month later they arrived. The sandhills migrated back to the Necedah NWR in spring 2001, returning to the exact spot where they had departed from the previous October.

If the sandhill cranes could do it, thought the U.S.-Canadian team, so could the whooping cranes. Following much the same script as that used for the sandhills, ten whooping crane chicks arrived at the Necedah NWR on July 10, 2001, via private plane. One of the chicks died during a routine health check, and another was transferred to the Audubon Zoo in New Orleans after it was found to have a wing abnormality. The remaining eight chicks, like astronauts preparing for a launch, had to pass a rigorous medical examination and then set about training with their handlers and the ultralight. As their muscles got stronger, the whooping cranes followed the ultralight on longer flights over the Wisconsin countryside. On October 17 the ultralight headed toward Florida with eight whooping cranes following close behind. The media covered the trip extensively, and former President Jimmy Carter and his wife, Rosalyn, honored the migration team with a visit on November 17. Bad weather and strong headwinds forced the migration team to spend twenty-two days on the ground, and even when the birds were in flight, there were days when the weather, including unusual warmth in Florida, slowed progress. One night, high winds

blew over the portable pen that housed the whooping cranes, and one escaped only to be killed when it collided with a power line. Another whooping crane was not adept at following the ultralight and had to be trucked from stop to stop. On December 3 the seven whooping cranes arrived in Crystal River, Florida, to a major welcoming event. Two days later, they were flown to the Chassahowitzka NWR. In the end the 1,228-mile trip was completed in fifty days and required twenty-six stops (more than thirty-five private landowners had offered their property for use as stopover sites).

Unfortunately, bobcats killed two of the whooping cranes soon after their arrival at the Chassahowitzka NWR. Efforts were then intensified to ensure that the remaining five cranes roosted each night either in water or within a large, protective, open-topped pen. As a result these five birds successfully survived the winter, adapted to local habitats, and on April 9, 2002, began their first northbound migration. The flock flew approximately 220 miles in seven hours on the first day of their return flight, exactly along the target route, heading toward their fledging area at the Necedah NWR. The timing of the whooping crane departure was remarkable because it coincided with the migration north of the whooping cranes at the Aransas NWR in Texas. Four of the whooping cranes returned to the Necedah NWR on April 19, 2002, at 6:37 P.M., landing within 0.5 mile of their training site. They covered the 1,175-mile return migration in only eleven days, even with several flightless days due to poor weather. Biologists tracked the cranes via radio and satellite transmitters on the birds' legs. Daily flights lasted six to eight hours and averaged more than 200 miles per day. They shaved 53 miles off the 1,228-mile fall migration by flying directly over large cities such as Chicago. The ultralight had to

navigate around major cities during the trip
south. Ground crews also relied on the satellite
transmitters and a fixed-wing aircraft to assist
with locating the birds when they migrated. One
female whooping crane separated from the
returning flock in Tennessee on the sixth day of
the migration and was tracked separately as she
returned. She completed the migration exactly
two weeks later than the other four cranes,
returning to the Necedah NWR on May 3, 2002.

This historic project was a great success, and
there is now a new migratory whooping crane
population in the eastern United States. How
these young birds followed their foster parent, an
ultralight aircraft, for fifty days, stopping at
twenty-six separate locations in farm fields down
to Florida, and then returned on their own,
unaided, flying a direct route back to the same
location in Wisconsin, is as incredible as it is mysterious. There is still a lot we don't understand
about bird migration. The whooping crane class of
2003 will hopefully provide fifteen to eighteen
more birds to repeat the southward migration with
the ultralights. The Whooping Crane Eastern
Partnership set an ambitious recovery goal for the
new migratory flock of 125 birds by 2020, including at least twenty-five breeding pairs.

During the 1960s and 1970s,
the refuge system added 140
refuges. In a move reminiscent of
Theodore Roosevelt's creation of
refuges just before leaving the
presidency, President Eisenhower
added to the refuge system on the
eve of relinquishing the reins of
power to John F. Kennedy in
1961. Lands set aside by
Eisenhower, although not as
extensive in terms of the number
of refuges created, were stupen-
dous for their sheer size. In late
1960 Interior Secretary Fred
Seaton announced the creation of
the 9-million-acre Arctic and
3-million-acre Clarence Rhode
NWRs in Alaska. "The great
diversity of vegetation and topog-
raphy in this compact area,"
Seaton said, "together with its relatively undisturbed condition, led
to its selection as the most suitable opportunity for protecting it
as one of our remaining wildlife
and wilderness frontiers."

The creation of the Arctic
NWR, in particular, was the
result of years of efforts by conservationists,
including George Collins, Lowell Sumner,
Supreme Court Justice William O. Douglas, and
Olaus and Margaret Murie, who spearheaded a
campaign that mobilized numerous organizations
and individuals to lobby on behalf of protecting
this magnificent reservoir of wild America.
Sumner saw in the Arctic wilderness a "freedom
to continue, unhindered and forever if we are
willing, the particular story of Planet Earth
unfolding here . . . where its native creatures can
still have freedom to pursue their future, so dis-

tant, mysterious." Decades later, this mysterious land that seemed so far away and peaceful would become the centerpiece of perhaps the fiercest and certainly the longest-lasting political battle ever to confront the refuge system.

In 1963 the Merritt Island NWR was created in the shadow of NASA's John F. Kennedy Space Center, Cape Canaveral, Florida. Donated to the refuge system by NASA, Merritt Island's 140,000 acres contain habitat for over 1,500 species of wildlife, including twenty-one state and federal threatened and endangered species. Merritt

Island adjoins Canaveral National Seashore, and together they include a 43-mile barrier island, the longest stretch of undeveloped beach along Florida's Atlantic coast and one of the most important nesting grounds for loggerhead, leatherback, and green sea turtles.

In 1969 the Mason Neck NWR in Virginia was added to the refuge system to provide habitat for the endangered bald eagle. When the Second Continental Congress officially adopted the bald eagle as the national emblem of the United States, it was still common in the wild.

John F. Kennedy Space Center launch pad as seen from the Merritt Island NWR, Florida.

RIGHT: A field of coneflowers at the Atchafalaya NWR, Louisiana.

By the mid-1960s, however, the population of this majestic raptor in the lower forty-eight states had dwindled to fewer than five hundred pairs. At the time there was one active nest on Mason Neck, a boot-shaped peninsula jutting into the Potomac River, 18 miles south of Washington, D.C. That is why, in 1965, when Elizabeth S. Hartwell heard of plans to develop a "satellite city" on Mason Neck, she leaped into action. How, she wondered, could anyone build on this beautiful piece of land, especially when it provided habitat for the endangered national symbol? Over the next year Hartwell and a local citizen's group that she helped form worked tirelessly to get local and federal officials to pay attention to Mason Neck and its potential role in eagle recovery efforts. Wildlife inventories were produced, telegrams were sent, briefings were held, and various media outlets picked up the story. These efforts paid off. In 1966 preserving Mason Neck became a top priority at the Department of the Interior. Then the Virginia

voters approved a bond to pay for purchasing part of Mason Neck as a state park. When the developers subsequently shelved their building plans, the Nature Conservancy, tipped off by Hartwell, bought nearly all of Mason Neck and later sold parts of it to the state for a park and to the Interior as an addition to the refuge system.

Mason Neck now has three active bald eagle nests and provides roosting habitat for sixty eagles. The refuge continues to play an important role in the eagle's resurgence and is part of the reason nearly 6,500 pairs are in the lower forty-eight. The eagles and all the wildlife and people who benefit from Mason Neck have Hartwell and her fellow activists to thank. As has been the case so many times, it was the power of passionate private citizens that enabled the refuge system to grow.

At the John Heinz NWR at Tinicum, along the many trails that wind through the largest remaining freshwater tidal wetland in Pennsylvania, one can look up and see the skyline of Philadelphia. When the Swedes, Dutch,

Waterfowl at sunrise at the Montezuma NWR New York. In the 1800s Peter Clark, a New York City physician, named his marshland estate Montezuma after the Aztec emperor. Apparently, Clark had become enamored with the name on a trip to Mexico, where Aztec history and cultural influence run deep. When the estate was made into a refuge in 1938, the traditional name of the area was kept.

and English first settled the area in the mid-1660s, the tidal wetlands spanned nearly 6,000 acres, but almost immediately the inevitable diking and draining made way for farming and grazing. Continued development and urbanization reduced the wetlands to a couple of hundred acres by the middle of the twentieth century, and in 1969 even that remnant was threatened by a proposal to route Interstate 95 through it. Years of lawsuits, injunctions, and public hearings and lobbying by public and private groups led to I-95 being rerouted just to the east of the wetlands. Then, in 1972, Congress authorized the creation of the Tinicum National Environmental Center to include the remaining wetlands and some of the surrounding land. The center, already a part of the refuge system, was renamed the John Heinz NWR in 1991 to honor the late senator from Pennsylvania whose efforts

had helped preserve Tinicum marsh.

The John Heinz NWR is a study in contrasts. Nearly three hundred species of birds have been sighted there, including thirty-five species of warblers. Active management, including diking and dredging, has created productive habitat for migratory waterfowl, as well as fish, reptiles, and aquatic vegetation. Students and other visitors take advantage of the wide range of educational programs offered. At the same time the John Heinz NWR suffers from many of the problems that face other urban areas that have been subject to intense development. Oil pipelines have long been running through and around the refuge, which is not surprising since an oil company formerly owned much of the land on which it sits. In February 2000 a 24-inch pipeline owned by Sunoco sprang a leak 6 feet under the refuge, sending a little more than 170,000 gallons of crude oil into a large pond, while another 18,000 gallons soaked into the soil. A massive cleanup effort was undertaken, and the refuge is healing itself with time.

But crude oil is not the only contaminant of concern at the John Heinz NWR. For many years there were industrial facilities in the area, including two sanitary landfills and an incinerator.

LEFT: The John Heinz NWR, Tinicum, Pennsylvania. Philadelphia's skyline can be seen in the distance.

Cooperative farmer harvesting corn at the Bombay Hook NWR, New Jersey.

Bottomland hardwood forest at the Felsenthal NWR, Arkansas.

Although these have long been closed, much of the wastes that they handled remained behind. Some of those wastes, including PCBs, heavy metals, and dioxins, have percolated through the soil, into the water, and into the food chain of which the wildlife in the refuge is a part. In June 2001 the U.S. Environmental Protection Agency determined that the area was so contaminated that it placed the lower Darby Creek, which flows into the refuge, and some of the surrounding lands on the list of the most dangerous hazardous waste sites in the country. It will probably be ten to fifteen years before the site is cleaned up. In the meantime, although the Environmental Protection Agency believes that the site doesn't threaten public health, visitors to the refuge have been warned not to eat any fish caught in the creek.

The John Heinz NWR was established to educate people about the environment, but for most of its existence, it didn't have an educational facility to carry out its charge. There simply wasn't any money. Then, in 1993, a quiet, unassuming, friendly man named Antonio "Tony" Cusano, who lived less than 2 miles away from the refuge and used to take walks there with his dog, died at the age of eighty-five. He had worked in the switchgear shop at the Philadelphia General Electric plant, lived frugally, and saved and invested his money wisely. In his will he left $2.47 million to the Department of the Interior. According to the executor of his estate, Greg Mallon, Cusano's choice was influenced by both his love of animals and the country that had been so good to him and his family, which had emigrated from Italy to Pittsburgh, where Tony was born. Mallon arranged with Pennsylvania congressman Curt Weldon, an ardent supporter of the refuge system, to have the money used to build an environmental education facility at the John Heinz NWR. The National Fish and Wildlife Foundation raised matching funds that nearly doubled Cusano's bequest, and Congress provided additional funding. On January 20, 2001, the 14,000-square-foot Cusano Environmental Education Facility opened to the public—a beautiful and important tribute to a generous and much remembered man.

The Felsenthal NWR, established in 1975 in southeastern Arkansas, encompasses 65,000 low-lying acres of swamps, rivers, sloughs, and lakes surrounded by a bottomland hardwood community that rises gradually to an upland forest. It is one of a chain of refuges dotting the Mississippi flyway and is used by a great diversity of migratory bird species, including hooded mergansers, king rails, lesser scaup, black-billed cuckoos, gadwalls, and the endangered red-cockaded woodpecker. One of the techniques used by refuge staff to improve the habitat for migratory waterfowl is called green-tree reservoir management. By carefully timing the flooding of bot-

tomland hardwood forest communities, refuge staff can increase available waterfowl habitat. Each winter, when the 15,000-acre Felsenthal Pool is flooded, it more than doubles in size to 36,000 acres, making it the largest green-tree reservoir in the world.

SEARCHING FOR DIRECTION

During the 1960s and 1970s the refuge system was following two paths. On the one hand it was growing, and legislative changes were further defining its responsibilities and expanding its reach. But at the same time many of the stresses and strains evident in the 1950s were compounded, and new ones were added. The problems facing the refuge system were captured by two task force studies separated by more than ten years. Stewart Udall, secretary of the interior, commissioned the first study in 1966. He asked his Advisory Board on Wildlife Management to study "what the National Wildlife Refuge System should be, if it could be rounded out, filled in or otherwise completed to include all that our national wildlife lands and waters should include or, conversely, need not or should not include." A. Starker Leopold, a professor of zoology at the University of California and son of Aldo Leopold, chaired the board. Two other members of the board were Ira Gabrielson, former head of the Bureau of Biological Survey, and Clarence Cottam, former assistant director of the Fish and Wildlife Service. In early 1969 the "Leopold committee" delivered a troubling

Sunset at the Bowdoin NWR, Montana.

159

Ghost crab on the beach at the St. Vincent NWR, Florida.

RIGHT: An endangered red-cockaded woodpecker at its nest hole bringing food for young at the Piedmont NWR, Georgia.

report on the health of the refuge system and issued a clarion call for improved management. Noting that the growth of the refuge system had been opportunistic, the report stated that although "There is no ambiguity regarding the desire or intent of Congress to perpetuate the [refuge system]. . . . What is still lacking, however, is a clear statement of policy or philosophy as to what the [refuge system] . . . should be and what are the logical tenets of its future development." Then in a single paragraph the committee painted a picture of why managing the refuge system and setting its course for the future was so difficult.

Nearly everyone has a slightly different view of what the refuge system is, or should be. Most duck hunters view the refuges as an essential cog in the perpetuation of their sport. Some see the associated public shooting grounds as the actual site of their sport. A few resent the concentration of birds in the refuges and propose general hunting to drive the birds out. Bird watchers and protectionists look upon the refuges as places to enjoy the spectacle of

masses of water birds, without disturbance by hunters or by private landowners; they resent any hunting at all. State fish and game departments are pleased to have the federal budget support wildlife areas in their states but want maximum public hunting and fishing on these areas. The General Accounting Office in Washington seems to view the refuges as units of a duck factory that should produce a fixed quota of ducks per acre or of bird days per duck stamp dollar. The Bureau of Outdoor Recreation sees the refuge system as 29 million acres of public playgrounds. All of these views are valid, to a point. Yet the National Wildlife Refuge System cannot be all things to all people. In America of the future, what are likely to be the highest social values that the refuges can serve?

The committee could have easily added to this list that some viewed the refuges as sources of timber, oil, gas, and land to be used for grazing and farming. The refuge system was being pushed and pulled in so many directions that it is not surprising that Secretary Udall needed assistance in getting it back on course or, more accurately, defining a clear course in the first place. The balance of the committee's report presented a thorough analysis of the problems facing the system, including insufficient funding to purchase increasingly expensive refuge lands before they succumbed to development, the absence of an orderly plan to guide the acquisition of new refuges, inadequate attention to the needs of wildlife beyond waterfowl, the neglect of big-game refuges, and threats to refuges posed by the "invasion by government agencies with higher rights of eminent domain." On this last issue the committee pointed to the recent decision by the Atomic Energy Commission to detonate an atomic bomb underneath Amchitka Island, a part of the Aleutian Islands NWR in Alaska and a major breeding area for the northern sea otter herd. "Project Longshot" took place in 1965 and was followed up by plans for five more detonations in the same area, some powerful enough to destroy major parts of the island and the wildlife in the vicinity. "Amchitka has been converted from a wildlife refuge," the committee declared, "to an atomic testing ground without the benefit of democratic process and over the objections" of the governor of Alaska.

At the end of its report, the committee laid out eleven recommendations. It urged the secretary to expand the refuge system in general, especially the number of migratory waterfowl refuges, develop long-range acquisition plans, increase research on refuges, and find additional sources of funding for land purchases. The committee also recommended that "plans for the development and management of individual refuges should include preservation and restoration of natural ecosystems [including all species of animals and plants] along with the primary management objective." Although the committee noted that refuges are for people as well as for animals and argued that the public uses of refuges, such as hunting, fishing, and general

recreation, should continue, the committee made it clear that such public uses should be allowed only when the primary purpose of the refuge is not placed in jeopardy. "Patterns of public use must be rigorously controlled . . . to minimize inappropriate activities," stated the report, and such use "should be managed to prevent undue disturbance of birds and mammals or interference with their welfare."

While the committee's report offered broad policies and philosophical arguments for managing the refuge system of the future, it suffered a bit from the same ailment that the report itself had ascribed to the refuge system as a whole—being all things to all people. The report still left unanswered the fundamental question of how, at the practical level, the refuge system should be managed so as to accommodate all the competing interests and objectives the system was supposed to represent. Broad pronouncements of the need to "protect the primary purposes of the refuge, to emphasize natural values, and to minimize inappropriate activities" were welcome, but what did they mean for the ground? Whatever limitations the report had, it did serve to focus the debate over the refuge system and made it clearer than ever before that despite the many legitimate uses of refuge lands the primary purpose of having a refuge system in the first place was to ensure the health of wildlife species, for without healthy wildlife almost all of the other uses of the system would come to naught. As the transmittal letter for the report stated, "The thrust of our argument is that in managing refuge units for their primary objectives . . . we purposefully guard and restore the broadest possible spectrum of wildlife values."

Ten years later, another NWR study task force, consisting of notables in the field of environmental and wildlife management and policy, submitted its findings and recommendations, many of which were disturbingly similar to those

Orb weaver spider and zigzag silk band at web's hub at the Petit Manan NWR, Maine.

RIGHT: Snowy owl wintering at the Sachuest Point NWR, Rhode Island.

The task force also recommended adopting the following mission statement: "The special mission of the National Wildlife Refuge System is to provide, preserve, restore and manage a national network of lands and waters sufficient in size, diversity and location to meet society's needs for areas where the widest possible spectrum of benefits associated with wildlife and wildlands is enhanced and made available." This statement echoes the Leopold report and, like that report, contained the seeds of its own undoing. Greenwalt, who was asked to comment on the report, noted that although mission statements had to have broad implications out of necessity, "there is room for interpretation and potential misunderstanding in this one." He continued, "'society's needs' is a broad statement that must be clearly conditioned . . . by the idea that the units of the National Wildlife Refuge System are intended to meet *wildlife* needs and through them the needs of society." Despite Greenwalt's misgivings, the mission statement was ultimately adopted with the caveat that "nothing should assume an 'equally important' role with the basic requirements necessary for the well-being of fish and wildlife resources."

The task force's report ended with a warning and call for action.

> Pressures to develop or degrade refuges for economic gain are growing exponentially. . . . developers cast increasingly longing eyes on resources in refuges. Energy is probably the most notable case in point, but the example is no less valid for agriculture, water development or mineral extraction. . . . clamor has grown to hasten development of energy resources. In some cases this has been translated as a mandate for development regardless of ensuing environmental consequences. This philosophy and approach should not be applied to the refuge system.
>
> The refuge system must be a strong, viable, clearly identifiable unit which stands for protection of the environment against encroachment on the Nation's natural heritage. This task requires public, administration and legislative support. The . . . [refuge system] needs a powerful, united constituency to protect it from exploitation and inappropriate development. The refuge system will remain strong only to the degree that it remains intact and develops solid public support.

It is ironic that just a few short years after these words were penned, the refuge system came under an assault the likes of which hadn't been seen since the days of "Generous Doug" McKay.

13

GROWING AND LOSING GROUND

Ronald Reagan was elected president in 1980. During the campaign he had made it clear that he would practice a brand of conservation with a decidedly prodevelopment bias. He placed James Watt at the helm of the Department of the Interior, a lawyer who had cut his teeth on the land wars in the West, usually taking the side of commercial interests in their battles for access to public lands against environmentalists and, often, the government. To some at the Fish and Wildlife Service, the new leadership brought with it an us-versus-them mentality. One employee at the time said that "when they came in here, they didn't make any secret of the fact that they thought this outfit was flabby, lazy, and infested with protectionists. They had nothing but contempt for the whole operation."

The administration soon began pushing to expand the commercial uses of refuges. This move was not unprecedented. Various efforts to expand such uses had been attempted for decades, and in many cases those efforts were justified and in line with the philosophical and statutorily based perspective that refuges were dominant-use lands, on which other activities

The Kenai NWR, Alaska.

167

A forest wetland at the Moosehorn NWR, Maine. Moosehorn is one of the northernmost refuges in the Atlantic flyway, located on the U.S.-Canadian border. The name of this refuge is misleading because moose have antlers, not horns.

were clearly permissible as long as they were carried out in a manner that did not detract from the purposes for which the refuges were established. The Reagan administration's push for expanded commercial use, however, appeared to many to be more aggressive than most earlier such efforts.

In 1981 the Fish and Wildlife Service headquarters sent a memorandum to all refuge managers asking them to identify ways to develop refuge lands. "We have reconsidered the potential of the National Wildlife Refuge System for supporting expanded economic uses and have identified the following types . . . as examples of where a potential for expansion exists. . . . Haying . . . Timber Harvest . . . Trapping. . . . This assessment will not be constrained by the current level of funding and manpower." The response was, to say the

least, unenthusiastic. To many refuge managers the commercial use of the refuge system had already gone too far. The year the memorandum went out, for example, there were timber operations at 20 refuges, grazing at 98, farming at 127, haying at 58, trapping at 45, concessions at 35, and oil and gas development at 11.

Headquarters was not pleased, so it sent out a second memo in 1982 that labeled the response to the first memo as not satisfactory. It urged the refuge managers to look harder and develop more options. "We believe that there is the potential to expand economic uses in such areas as grazing, haying, farming, timber harvest, trapping, oil and gas extraction, small hydroelectric generation, concessions, commercial hunting and fishing. We believe that if you use innovation and creativity, and if necessary a redirection

Wild turkeys strutting at first light at the Karl Mundt NWR, South Dakota. This refuge is named after a South Dakota senator who had been a strong proponent of the Endangered Species Act. When established, the refuge's main purpose was to provide wintering habitat for bald eagles.

Tundra vista at the Yukon Delta NWR, Alaska. This refuge provides feeding habitat for 750,000 swans and geese, two million ducks, and one hundred million shore- and waterbirds.

RIGHT: Salmon drying in Eskimo fish camp at the Yukon Delta NWR, Alaska.

of your efforts, these as well as other uses can be expanded." The response this time was greater but still unenthusiastic. When the director of the Fish and Wildlife Service summarized the results of these efforts, he concluded that there was the potential to raise revenues on refuge lands from $6 million to $8 million a year by selling more merchantable timber.

Funding for the refuge system during the 1980s rose significantly some years, and fell in others, but continued to be anemic compared with need. On occasions where administration budget requests were unusually meager, congressional champions of the refuge system often stepped forward to up the amount. For example, in fiscal year 1983 the administration requested

$1.6 million from the Land and Water Conservation Fund for the refuge system; Congress appropriated $27.2 million. Despite the fiscal and administrative ups and downs, the refuge system continued to grow, with more than seventy refuges added during the decade. Unfortunately, all of the appropriations were for refuge acquisition and not for desperately needed operations and maintenance work. The state of the refuge system continued to decline.

On December 2, 1980, just before Reagan assumed office, the refuge system took an enormous leap forward. With the passage of the Alaska National Interest Lands Conservation Act of 1980 (ANILCA), nine new refuges were added to the system, and six existing Alaskan refuges were expanded, altogether adding 53.7 million acres and nearly tripling the size of the refuge system. The act also set aside roughly another 50 million acres as national parks, forests, and conservation areas. It was the culmination of decades of fierce and impassioned debate inside and outside the halls of Congress and the White House, involving a huge number of organizations and individuals. The biggest battle was over development and how setting aside massive tracts of federal lands would impact future options for everything ranging from mining to oil and gas exploration. Former President Jimmy Carter, who signed ANILCA one month after being defeated for a second term by Reagan, said about the historic law, "I don't believe there has ever been an issue so contentious in the U.S. Congress that involved more powerful interests marshaled against one another."

It is hard to comprehend the magnitude of ANILCA's impact on the refuge system, especially when considered in conjunction with the massive amount of refuge acreage in Alaska that had already been protected prior to the act. Rather than managing specific species and pursuing resource restoration, refuge workers in Alaska manage entire ecosystems. The goal is not so much the improvement of habitat as it is maintenance of the pristine conditions that already exist. Monitoring the condition of the refuges, by necessity, is often done by plane. The Arctic NWR alone extends over 19.6 million acres, sits astride the Brooks Range, and provides habitat for virtually undisturbed populations of polar bears, grizzly bears, black bears, caribou, wolves, migratory waterfowl, and other species, leading some to call the refuge America's Serengeti. Many of the refuges have native villages in them or nearby, and special provisions are made to enable the natives to continue to live off of the land and pursue traditional gathering activities.

The passage of ANILCA did not end the fighting over refuges in Alaska; it just moved it into a newer, even more combative phase. One

Fireweed along the coastal plain at the Arctic NWR, Alaska.

RIGHT: Ice along the shore of the Beaufort Sea at the Arctic NWR, Alaska.

of the last-minute compromises included in the bill involved the 1.5-million-acre coastal plain of the Arctic refuge. Ever since 1968, when the Atlantic Richfield Company discovered enormous oil deposits on Alaskan state land in Prudhoe Bay on the North Slope, the potential value of Alaskan real estate skyrocketed as many dreamed of finding similar deposits elsewhere in the state. One of those areas was the coastal

plain. Opponents of drilling for oil, including many environmental groups, wanted to designate the coastal plain, along with another 8 million acres of the refuge, as wilderness, effectively protecting it from development, but others, including many oil companies, were against such a designation and instead wanted to explore the feasibility of drilling on that land. The deal that was struck involved two sections of the law.

Section 1002 left off the wilderness designation for the coastal plain and required the Department of the Interior to submit a report to Congress on the oil and gas potential of the plain and how such activities might impact wildlife and its habitats. And Section 1003 prohibited any leasing, development, or oil or gas production in the Arctic refuge unless Congress authorized such actions. The battle lines were drawn between those who wanted to drill and those who didn't, and each group set out to prove its case.

In 1987 the Interior submitted the final 1002 report to Congress. Although the report noted that oil and gas development could have significant impacts on resources, including the Porcupine caribou herd, wilderness, and water quality, it argued that these impacts could be mitigated and, anyway, were outweighed by the energy and security benefits. The report concluded that the entire coastal plain should be open to oil and gas exploration. Given the Reagan administration's extremely strong prodevelopment philosophy, some viewed the report as being driven more by politics than facts.

Government agencies and private groups have written many subsequent reports on the oil and gas production in the coastal plain. Some have offered findings that lend support to arguments in favor of drilling, whereas others have not. And at times both sides of the debate have used the same reports to support different conclusions. Many of these reports, too, have been greeted with skepticism and claims that the findings were colored by political motivation rather than objective analysis. None of the reports have been conclusive, and certainly none have reduced the enormous tensions that exist between the proponents and opponents of drilling.

In 1998 the U.S. Geological Survey came out with one of the most important studies on the potential for oil production on the coastal plain. The report used old and new seismic and drilling data to determine how much oil might be recoverable from the area. Then in 2000 the survey used its updated data and recent oil prices to estimate oil recovery rates given different economic conditions. At a price of $24 per barrel, the survey concluded that there was a 95 percent chance of finding 1.9 billion barrels of economically recoverable oil under the coastal plain, a 50 percent chance of finding 5.3 billion barrels, and a 5 percent chance of finding 9.4 billion barrels.

Newly hatching tundra swans at
the Yukon Delta NWR, Alaska.

If the price per barrel were $16, then there would
be no economically recoverable oil in the area.
When these estimates were made, Americans
used roughly seven billion barrels of oil per year.
Therefore, another way to look at the findings is
that at $24 per barrel there might be a 50 percent
chance that the coastal plain could economically
produce enough oil to fulfill America's needs for
nine months. To some this is an impressive
amount well worth pursuing. To others the environmental costs of the pursuit vastly outweigh
any benefits that might accrue.

In late March 2002 the U.S. Geological
Survey came out with its *Arctic Refuge Coastal
Plain Terrestrial Wildlife Research Summaries*,
which analyzed the potential impacts of oil and
gas development on different wildlife species.
The report contained already published as well
as updated information, and it used five scenarios of oil and gas development to estimate
impacts. Although the report contained information on many species, most of the public's attention focused on the results for the famed
Porcupine caribou herd. The report indicated
that the "herd may be particularly sensitive to
development within the 1002 portion of the
calving ground" and that under the worst-case
scenario calf survival rates might fall by 8 percent. A controversy immediately ensued. Those
opposed to drilling pointed to the report as
offering further evidence that drilling must not
proceed. At the other end of the spectrum were
those who felt that the worst-case scenarios were
not likely to occur and that, even if they did, the
impacts were still relatively minor and could be
mitigated to some extent.

A week after the first report came out, the
U.S. Geological Survey issued a second report in
which two other development scenarios were
plugged into the caribou-calving model, ones
that were less extensive than the worst-case sce-

nario used in the initial report. This time, it was determined that calf survival rates would drop at most by 1.2 percent. The second report was greeted with even more controversy than the first. Many opponents of drilling argued that the second report, commissioned by the Secretary of the Interior Gale A. Norton, was merely an attempt to subvert the process. According to Charles Clusen, director of the Natural Resource Defense Council's Alaska Project, "They [the administration] didn't like the results of a 12-year study, so they ordered a new study to get the results they really wanted. This rush job should not be taken seriously." Others felt that this simply was not the case. To William Seitz, the U.S. Geological Survey's deputy regional director for Alaska, "the point is that oil development is not the end of the world for any of the species in the report. We've documented the importance of these habi-

tats at critical times, so you can work out a development scenario that avoids and protects them."

It is not surprising that additional studies and reports have done little to temper the debate over the future of the coastal plain. The gulf separating the two sides is as much a function of values as it is of facts, especially when the latter are often the subject of disagreement. How, for example, can one bridge the gap between people who view the Arctic refuge as simply a desert with snow and those who agree with former Supreme Court Chief Justice William D. Douglas, who pronounced many years ago that "this last American living wilderness must remain sacrosanct." Like the epic battle over the Hetch Hetchy dam in Yosemite National Park led by John Muir around the turn of the nineteenth century, the battle over the fate of the coastal plain has become a national cause

Crystal Springs at the Ash Meadows NWR, Nevada. In the 1960s and 1970s, many of the springs that feed Ash Meadows were diverted for agricultural use, leading to the extinction of the Ash Meadows killifish and the Longstreet springsnail. Concerned citizens and the Nature Conservancy focused their efforts on protecting Ash Meadows from further use and development, and in 1984 the Nature Conservancy bought 12,163 acres of land in the area, which was, in turn, sold to the Fish and Wildlife Service to create the refuge.

Houseboats at the White River NWR, Arkansas. No new permits for houseboats are being issued within the refuge, so when the lifetime leases held by the current owners of the houseboats expire, houseboats in White River will become a thing of the past.

RIGHT: Pollution along the coast at the Petit Manan NWR, Maine. Unfortunately, refuges have to confront and deal with many of the environmental problems that plague other areas of the country.

warmed, the waters receded, creating populations of species that were isolated from one another. Over many thousands of years the animals and plants in these small biotic islands, such as Ash Meadows, evolved along separate paths into new species. Today, the pools and seeps on the refuge are kept alive by fifteen major springs that feed the area with water that is estimated to be between eight thousand and twelve thousand years old, coming from a vast aquifer north of Las Vegas.

The Kilauea NWR was established in 1985 on the Hawaiian island of Kauai to protect one of the last remnant colonies of seabirds in Hawaii as well as the endangered Nene goose. Hawaii used to be home to enormous populations of seabirds, but with the introduction of predators such as dogs, cats, and mongooses, the seabirds suffered dramatically and today are relegated to nesting on steep cliffs, offshore rocks, and remote atolls where they are further protected by fences and predator control programs. Visitors can see a great range of wildlife, including red-footed boobies, Pacific golden plovers, Hawaiian monk seals, spinner dolphins, and humpback whales. Set on a promontory, the refuge's focal point is the retired Kilauea Lighthouse. Built in 1913 as an aid to commercial shipping, the light-

house played a key role in the first trans-Pacific flight between California and Hawaii by redirecting the two pilots of *The Bird of Paradise* who had gotten lost on their way to Honolulu. In 1979 the Kilauea Lighthouse was placed on the National Register of Historic Places and is now owned by the Fish and Wildlife Service.

A small number of refuges are in U.S. territories and possessions. One of the most spectacular of these is the Midway Atoll NWR, covering roughly 1,550 acres and located about 1,250 miles west-northwest of Honolulu in the midst of the Pacific Ocean. Around twenty-eight million years ago a volcanic island sat where Midway Atoll is today, the result of massive amounts of molten magma erupting through a "hot spot" in the earth's crust. Over vast stretches of time, the elements eroded the island, and its own weight caused it to slowly sink back into the ocean. As the island was getting smaller and sinking, coral reefs were being built up around the island's edges, and bits of coral, shells, and the skeletons of small marine organisms were deposited on the reef, eventually creating sandy spits and dunes and broader expanses of dry land. During the 1800s and early 1900s, various commercial concerns imported soil to expand the size of the atoll and allow for the building of structures and the planting of crops and trees. Today, Midway Atoll contains three islands—Sand, Eastern, and Spit—as well as a protective coral reef that surrounds the islands and is roughly 5 miles in diameter.

Midway Atoll is most famous for its role in the epic Battle of Midway in World War II, the decisive engagement of the war in the Pacific in which a relatively small contingent of U.S. ships, aircraft, and submarines used Midway Atoll as a base of operations in its successful fight against the larger Japanese fleet. Remnants of the atoll's illustrious military past can still be found on the island, including abandoned gun emplacements, pillboxes, airstrips, and radar buildings, many of which are designated as national historic landmarks. The U.S. Navy invited the Fish and Wildlife Service to establish an "overlay" refuge on the atoll in 1988, and when Midway's naval facility closed, the atoll was transferred to the Fish and Wildlife Service. As part of the effort to restore Midway's natural condition, the Fish and Wildlife Service worked with the navy to remove more than one hundred dilapidated buildings and numerous underground storage tanks and also to clean up contaminants resulting from military operations. Rats, an introduced species that posed a serious threat to bird eggs and chicks, were also eradicated. There is still more that needs to be done. For example, refuge staff and volunteers continue to work to control alien species of plants and replace them with native species.

The Midway Atoll NWR provides nesting habitat for nearly two million seabirds representing fifteen species. The most conspicuous are the albatrosses, or so-called gooney birds. Midway lays claim to the largest colony of Laysan albatrosses in the world and the second largest colony of black-footed albatrosses. And the lucky visitor can also spy a short-tailed albatross, which is called the golden gooney because of the color of the plumage on its head. The albatrosses share the atoll with many other birds, including brown noddies, white terns, bristle-thighed curlews, and white-tailed tropicbirds. The deep blue and turquoise waters surrounding the Midway Atoll NWR are teeming with life. Hawaiian spinner dolphins play in the surf. Endangered Hawaiian monk seals bask on the white sand beaches. Beautiful mollusks crawl along the bottom of sheltered lagoons. Reef fish flash all the colors of the rainbow as they dart in and around the coral reefs, while much larger pelagic fish, such as marlin and tuna, glide through the deeper waters not far from the edge of the reefs. Only a select few get to see the natural wonders of the Midway Atoll NWR. The Fish and Wildlife Service limits visitors to one hundred at a time, and they are transported to and from the atoll on a weekly Aloha Airlines flight originating in Honolulu.

Fourteen-month-old male
endangered Florida panther at
the Florida Panther NWR,
Florida.

Long, sleek, and beautiful, Florida panthers once roamed freely over the southeastern United States as rulers of their domain. Today, there are only thirty to fifty left, and their range is reduced to southern Florida. The Florida Panther NWR, established in 1989 and located near Naples, Florida, is helping this endangered species survive by providing critical habitat. The Florida panther is the state animal and a subspecies of cougar that goes by many names, including *mountain lion* and *puma,* which means "mighty magic animal" in the Quechua Indian language of Peru. The Seminole Indians of Florida call the panther simply *coo-wah-chobee,* or "big cat." Adult male Florida panthers have a large home territory and in a month can range over 200 square miles. The refuge, which covers 26,000 acres, is the core of the home range for several panthers and also serves as a travel corridor for many more as they move between other protected areas. A few female panthers have had litters and raised kittens on the refuge in recent years. The Florida Panther NWR is closed to all public use and access in order to protect the panther's habitat and minimize the chances of human interactions with this secretive and potentially dangerous animal.

At the end of the 1980s, the refuge system was still confronting serious problems. In 1987 the General Accounting Office (GAO) produced a report on refuge contamination. The report was prompted by problems at the Kesterson NWR in California that became big news nationwide in the mid-1980s. Selenium-rich agricultural water had drained onto the refuge and severely contaminated the wildlife there, leading to, among other things, a very high incidence of dead or deformed newborn waterfowl. The GAO report noted a Department of the Interior survey performed in 1985 that found that 85 of the 430 refuges are or may be contaminated by industrial, municipal, military, and other wastes. While the GAO report stated that the Interior's survey was useful, it also said that more studies would have to be undertaken before the full extent of contamination on refuges could be accurately known. In 1989 the GAO attacked the most vexing issue facing the refuge system—incompatible uses. More than twenty years after the compatibility standard became a statutory mandate, its implementation was still giving the refuge system heartburn. After evaluating questionnaire responses from 96 percent of the refuge managers, conducting case studies on sixteen refuges, and reviewing Fish and Wildlife Service policies and guidance, the GAO presented cause for alarm. The refuge managers reported that "activities they consider harmful to wildlife resources . . . are occurring on nearly 60 percent of the wildlife refuges." Among the activities cited were mining, water skiing, military air and ground exercises, grazing, and the use of off-road vehicles, airboats, and powerboats. The report concluded that "while the total effect of harmful uses on wildlife cannot be quantified, there is no doubt that the effect is negative." In 1990 a compatibility task group convened by the Fish and Wildlife Service delivered its report reviewing secondary uses on refuge lands. The findings echoed those of the GAO and found that many refuges were subject to one or more harmful uses.

14

TURNING THE REFUGE SYSTEM AROUND

By the early 1990s the refuge system had been asked to do so much for so long with so little that its success was truly a tribute to the hard work of its employees and their drive and ingenuity to make do in the face of inadequate financial support and, oftentimes, confusing and conflicting operational directives. But the success of the refuge system in the face of adversity paled in comparison with the success it could have if given the tools and support it deserved. Those who cared deeply about the refuges saw this disparity between reality and promise, and they redoubled their efforts to get the refuge system the resources it needed to do its job.

One of the most comprehensive efforts to evaluate where the refuge system was and what needed to be done to get it where it ought to be was undertaken by the nonprofit organization Defenders of Wildlife, which in 1992 issued a report titled *Putting Wildlife First: Recommendations for Reforming Our Troubled Refuge System.* It was prepared by the independent Commission on New Directions for the National Wildlife Refuge System. The commission was made up of eighteen well-known and respected

Freshwater wetland in fall at the Rice Lake NWR, Minnesota.

professionals in the fields of wildlife biology, management, and law, as well as citizen advocacy on behalf of wildlife. In scope and quality the report was a lineal descendant of the Leopold report and the 1979 NWR task force report that followed it. The picture painted by this report, however, was much grimmer than the ones offered by its predecessors. Decades of additional neglect had left their mark.

The introduction to the commission report is unequivocal.

Refuges are falling short of their potential and far short of meeting the urgent habitat needs of the nation's wildlife. Too many refuges are hamstrung by entrenched human uses that work against wildlife's well-being. Nearly all are threatened by neighboring land abuses or by contaminants moving downriver or downwind. The wildlife refuge collection as a whole languishes at the fringe of

public interest and thus suffers chronic fiscal starvation and administrative neglect.

The basic conclusions of the commission were equally straightforward. The refuge system lacked a clear legislative mandate and suffered from a variety of threats, including harmful uses and watershed degradation that "make some refuges little more than oases in a desert of urbanized, cropped, overgrazed, overlogged landscapes." The commission also argued that the Department of the Interior gave neither the Fish and Wildlife Service nor the refuge system the stature or financial support necessary to manage resource uses and limit or get rid of threats.

The commission offered a range of recommendations, including better defining the standards for determining compatibility of secondary uses, improving refuge planning, and expanding habitat acquisition. It also urged Congress to pass an organic act for the refuge system that set forth a clear and far-reaching mission for the refuge system. For this recommendation, in particular, the commission had the support of many other organizations and individuals who had long complained that without a strong organic act the refuge system would continue to lack focus and direction. Indeed, many organizations, including the Natural Resources Defense Council, the National Wildlife Federation, the Sierra Club, the Wilderness Society, the National Audubon Society, and others, were already on record in support of organic act legislation. The value of an organic act was much more than

symbolic. Academic research had shown what common sense would seem to indicate, namely, that organizations that have a clear statutory mission would derive benefits in terms of effectiveness and the ability to secure resources.

Throughout the mid-1990s the pressure for an organic act mounted. The approach of the centennial of the refuge system, on March 14, 2003, added to the sense of urgency. Certainly, the refuge system deserved clarity of purpose

after having provided this country with untold benefits for nearly a century. Then, on March 25, 1996, President William Clinton signed Executive Order 12996. It wasn't an organic act, but it did clarify the refuge system's mission and purpose and the acceptable public uses of refuges. In announcing the order Clinton said, "The history of the National Wildlife Refuge System is a story of untiring effort and timeless contributions from legions

LEFT: Rainbow trout in river raceway at Leavenworth National Fish Hatchery, Washington. This is one of the most sought after species for anglers on refuges.

Limestone cliffs along the Missouri River at the Big Muddy NWR, Missouri.

Bracket fungi on sugar maple at the Seney NWR, Michigan.

RIGHT, ABOVE: Raccoon at the Montezuma NWR, New York.

RIGHT, BELOW: Ring-necked pheasant at the Quivira NWR, Kansas.

of dedicated individuals and of government serving its people. Collectively, these efforts have culminated in what is unquestionably the largest and most outstanding wildlife conservation program in the world." Almost before the ink had dried on the order, the refuge system got its organic act in the form of the National Wildlife Refuge System Improvement Act of 1997, signed by President Clinton on October 9, 1997. It had taken nearly one hundred years, but finally the refuge system had clear, compelling, and inspiring marching orders. The refuge system's new mission statement placed wildlife first: "The mission of the National Wildlife Refuge System is to administer a national network of lands and waters for the conservation, management, and where appropriate, restoration of the fish, wildlife, and plant resources and their habitats within the United States for the benefit of present and future generations of Americans."

The act requires the monitoring of the refuge system's fish, wildlife, and plants and the implementation of steps necessary to maintain the system's biological integrity, diversity, and environmental health. The growth of the refuge system must be designed in a way that contributes to the conservation of ecosystems. To help ensure that the refuge system is managed properly, the act requires a comprehensive conservation plan for each refuge that must guide management decisions. The act recognizes six compatible wildlife-dependent uses of the system—hunting, fishing, wildlife observation and photography, and environmental education and interpretation. These are to be encouraged, but only when the refuge manager, using his or her professional judgment, determines such uses are compatible with the mission of the refuge system and the purposes for which the particular refuge was established. This determination is not made in a vacuum; the act requires public and interagency input on compatibility and other refuge management decisions.

The act created the framework for action, but it is up to the Fish and Wildlife Service to determine how the law will be applied. A critical step down this path took place in Keystone, Colorado, where the first-ever refuge system conference was held October 1998. That this was the first time the refuge system had ever drawn together representatives from all its units throughout the country was almost as amazing as the fact that it had taken nearly a century for the refuge system to get an organic act. Out of this historic meeting came the refuge system's

Magna Carta—forty-two vision statements detailing not only where the people who made the refuge system work wanted it to go but also how they planned to get it there. Appropriately enough, *Fulfilling the Promise* was both the theme of the conference and the name of the document containing the vision statements.

Fulfilling the Promise focuses on wildlife, habitat, people, and leadership. According to this document the refuge system will ensure that wildlife comes first by focusing its efforts on ecologically based objective setting, population and habitat monitoring, and adaptive management or, in other words, experimenting and being flexible so as to take advantage of changing ecosystem dynamics. As for the people, the refuge system must always keep in mind that one of the greatest resources for wildlife conservation is the support of and understanding of the citizenry.

Through appropriate public uses of refuges, improved educational programs, new alliances with community groups, and an active outreach program, the refuge system can keep the public in touch, inspired, and informed. Environmental education programs, in particular, must be a major focus of activity on refuges. Finally, *Fulfilling the Promise* points out that without effective leadership the visions for wildlife, habitat, and people will be impossible to achieve. To that end the refuge system should endeavor to hire the best people, provide them with clear guidance, and establish an esprit de corps within the refuge system's ranks. The Fish and Wildlife Service immediately took steps to carry out the intent of *Fulfilling the Promise,* and it has made great progress. According to James Kurth, deputy chief of the National Wildlife Refuge System, "For the first time in a great many years we are implementing new policies to strengthen the Refuge System and that is so important." This includes policies for administering the compatibility test, protecting biological integrity, and performing comprehensive conservation planning.

The heady optimism and excitement resulting from the passage of the organic act and the steps taken toward *Fulfilling the Promise* could not hide the problems still facing the refuge system. In the late 1990s and early in the next century, longstanding frustrations and concerns about organization boiled to the surface. The fundamental question was what type of structure would enable the refuge system to be most effectively managed and to achieve the organizational clout and positioning it needed to successfully battle for resources. Should the refuge system be a separate bureau or service within the Department of the Interior, like the National Park Service, or should it remain a division within the Fish and Wildlife Service, perhaps with a higher profile?

Black-crowned night-heron feeding at the Fish Springs NWR, Utah.

Beaver dam at the Canaan Valley NWR, West Virginia. In 1994 Canaan Valley became the nation's five hundredth NWR. The valley sits at 3,200 feet above sea level, making it the highest valley of its size east of the Rocky Mountains.

The refuge supports nearly six hundred species of plants and three hundred species of wildlife, including the threatened Cheat Mountain salamander and the endangered West Virginia northern flying squirrel.

Ever since the Leopold report, there had been calls for organizational restructuring. In 1992 the commission that prepared *Putting Wildlife First* recommended that the refuge system be reorganized into a new structure that would strengthen refuge programs, increase awareness of the refuge system, and give it autonomy in planning, budgeting, and research. The commission noted that there were a number of ways to accomplish this, including giving the head of the refuge system a higher position within the Fish and Wildlife Service or taking the refuges out of the Fish and Wildlife Service and creating a new wildlife refuge service. In 1999 the National Audubon Society decided that a new agency was the way to go and launched a campaign to create one within the Department of the Interior. An Audubon Society public service announcement proclaimed, "Here's a once-in-a-lifetime chance to actually create a species," and then went on to call for a national wildlife refuge service. The society argued that the government had been ignoring the refuge system and that the Fish and Wildlife

Service was overburdened, having to administer many diverse programs, all of which were competing for resources. "In practice," the society claimed, "this limits the Service's ability to promote the refuge system to the Congress and the American people, and to provide adequate funding and leadership attention to refuges."

The debate over organization has been emotional and intense. The Fish and Wildlife Service has focused a great amount of thought and energy on the issue and has concluded that necessary changes can be made within the existing structure of the refuge system. In testimony before Congress in 2000, former Fish and Wildlife Service Director Jamie Rappaport Clark pointedly said, "I am completely opposed to recent proposals to tear apart the U.S. Fish and Wildlife Service by removing the National Wildlife Refuge System. This irresponsible and ill-considered suggestion would destroy the only federal agency dedicated solely to fish and wildlife conservation and would be detrimental to furthering comprehensive conservation efforts

LEFT: Waterfowl and ibis at sunset at the Lacassine NWR, Louisiana. Lacassine supports one of the largest concentrations of wintering waterfowl in the entire refuge system, with upwards of three hundred thousand ducks and eighty thousand geese.

Refuge workers installing a water control pipe at the Back Bay NWR, Virginia. Reflecting on the critical importance of refuge system employees, former Fish and Wildlife Service Director Lynn Greenwalt said, "And it is your obligation to . . . move forward . . . in a way that does not denigrate, dilute or diminish in the slightest degree that which came before you, because many thousands of men and women gave their careers, and some even gave their lives, for what you are working toward—saving dirt."

Dickcissel singing in a meadow clearing at the Clarence Cannon NWR, Missouri.

RIGHT: Winter cottonwoods and storm clouds in first light at the Squaw Creek NWR, Missouri.

nationwide." One of the major concerns is that by creating a separate service, important interconnections between the refuge system and other parts of the Fish and Wildlife Service, such as the endangered species program, will be damaged. In an effort to give the refuge system more visibility within the Fish and Wildlife Service and more of a voice, the position of chief of the National Wildlife Refuge System was created in 2000; the person holding that position reports directly to the head of the Fish and Wildlife Service.

The debate over organization is not over. In 2001 the Blue Goose Alliance, a national not-for-profit organization, incorporated in New Mexico. Its goal is to establish the National Wildlife Refuge Service as a separate agency within the Department of the Interior. The alliance is composed mainly of past refuge system employees, including many that were at the top of the refuge system's management hierarchy. The alliance believes that recent organizational changes within the refuge system are more cosmetic than real and that only separate agency status will enable the refuge system to attain its full potential. Of course, those who support the reorganization efforts and those who want a new agency share the same goal, namely, ensuring that the refuge

The White Bluffs at Hanford
Reach National Monument/
Saddle Mountain NWR,
Washington. Designated a
national monument in June
2000, it protects the only free-
flowing nontidal stretch of the
Columbia River.

RIGHT: Prairie pothole country
at the Lostwood NWR, North
Dakota.

system is vibrant and strong. They just disagree
over the means of achieving that goal.

The refuge system also still faces problems
that go well beyond organizational matters.
Many of these are highlighted in a report issued
by the National Audubon Society in early 2001
titled *Refuges in Crisis,* which focuses on ten
refuges that are "jeopardized by imminent
threats and are failing to protect bird species that
are federally-listed as threatened or endangered
or are included in Audubon's WatchList of
species that could be headed for extinction." The
report cites five major threats: habitat loss, invasive species, harmful public uses, water pollution, and limited water supplies. This list is par-

ticularly interesting because it shows that many
threats to the refuges come from sources outside
of the refuges' borders and are often difficult or
impossible to resolve. For example, pesticides
and fertilizers used in lands surrounding refuges
often contaminate the waters on which the
wildlife in refuges depends. The report also notes
that many refuges compete with other users for
limited sources of water, and making matters
worse, refuges often only have tenuous legal
rights to use the water in the first place. An
external threat not listed in the report is air pollution. Like water, air does not respect the
artificial boundaries at the edge of refuges, and
there are many refuges where the air that the

plants, animals, and visitors breathe is polluted. One of the refuges profiled is the Sonny Bono Salton Sea NWR in California, where migratory waterfowl and other bird species were cited as being threatened by water pollution from agricultural drainage, water shortages due to increasing demand from neighboring states and other parts of California, and invasive fish species that spread disease and could harm fish-eating birds. The report also argues that the commercial harvesting of horseshoe crabs at the Monomoy NWR in Massachusetts endangered local crab populations and also placed at serious risk shorebirds, including the red knot, that rely on horseshoe crab eggs for sustenance. The refuges in the report were not the only ones in crisis, just some of those in the worst straits.

Of particular concern to the Audubon Society was how the problems besetting the refuge system might negatively impact recreation and tourism. Noting that "more than 100 million Americans spend $96 billion each year pursuing wildlife-related recreation such as birdwatching, hunting, and fishing," the report concluded that "without a healthy National Wildlife Refuge System, local economies across the nation will suffer." The potential for damage was borne out by a Fish and Wildlife Service study in 1995 that showed that recreational visits to refuges generated more than $400 million in sales for local communities. At the Chincoteague NWR in Virginia, for example, the economic activity of more than one million visitors created almost 3 percent of the surrounding county's earned income for the year, and within the smaller area of Chincoteague's zip code, nearly a third of all jobs were attributable to refuge visitation.

The most serious problem facing the refuge system is a lack of funding. The accumulation of fiscal neglect has left the refuge system in a deep hole, and it still has a long way to climb out.

Gone begging are projects, maintenance work, and other initiatives that affect nearly every aspect of the refuge system's operations, including wildlife research, habitat restoration and improvement, educational outreach, and building upkeep.

In late 2001 the Cooperative Alliance for Refuge Enhancement (CARE) issued a report titled *Shortchanging America's Wildlife,* in which it claimed that the refuge system is underfunded "to the tune of $2 billion," a number that is in line with Fish and Wildlife Service estimates. An effective advocate for the refuge system, CARE is made up of twenty influential and diverse conservation and recreational organizations, ranging from the Wilderness Society and Defenders of Wildlife to the National Rifle Association and Safari Club International. The report doesn't mince words

> In spite of its critical role in conserving America's wildlife over the last 100 years, the Refuge System is in danger of being unable to do the same in the next 100 years. Severe funding and staffing shortfalls have led to the decline of refuge habitats and wildlife populations, aging facilities and infrastruc-

Immature red-headed woodpecker storing an acorn for winter at the Necedah NWR, Wisconsin.

MIDDLE: Singing female yellow-headed blackbird at the Bowdoin NWR, Montana.

FAR RIGHT: Canada geese on a coastal wetland at sunset in the Blackwater NWR, Maryland. Blackwater was established in 1933. Before that, much of its land supported a fur farm, with muskrats being the primary "crop." It was also the location of logging and other agricultural uses. Walking through the refuge, one can still see the evidence of these activities in the form of drainage furrows and ditches as well as relatively young stands of trees.

coffers dry? We are turning a source of national pride into a source of national shame. It is time to do the right thing."

While the main source of funding for the refuge system has been and will continue to be congressional appropriations, there is another source of support that is critically important. Ever since the refuge system began, it has benefited greatly from the assistance of people who, motivated by their love of wildlife, have volunteered their valuable time and energy to help maintain and improve refuges in and around their communities. Although they work for free, volunteers provide immeasurable economic benefits through their in-kind efforts that, in effect, help make up for the shortfalls in traditional refuge funding. Roughly thirty-six thousand volunteers, more than ten times the number of refuge system employees, perform an impressive 20 percent of all the work on refuges nationwide. The refuge system, as well as the American people, are indebted to this productive group of volunteers for providing an extremely valuable national service.

One of the most successful volunteer groups is the Friends of Blackwater NWR in Maryland, a

nonprofit organization established in 1987. The Friends of Blackwater count among its members more than eight hundred individuals, organizations, companies, and agencies that are all dedicated to helping the refuge carry out its educational, interpretive, and public use missions. The friends run the Eagle's Nest Bookstore, located at the refuge's visitor center, and all the proceeds from that venture go toward purchasing needed refuge supplies and services not covered by the refuge system's budget. Members of the Friends of Blackwater have funded exhibits at the visitor

center and the planting of thousands of trees, constructed photo blinds and canoeing-kayaking trails, administered the Refuge Hunt Program, and published a manual to help elementary schoolteachers take advantage of learning opportunities at the refuge. The Friends of Blackwater also produce a first-rate newsletter, *Blackwater Tidelines,* and maintain an exceptionally informative and fun Web site that it developed.

The National Wildlife Refuge Association (NWRA), a national membership organization dedicated solely to protecting and perpetuating the refuge system, spurred the creation of friends' groups in 1996. That year, the association launched an initiative to increase the number of friends' groups through training, networking, and financial support. A few years later, the creation of friends' groups got another boost in the form of the National Wildlife Refuge System Volunteer and Community Partnership Enhancement Act of 1998. The act authorizes funding for the establishment of volunteer programs at refuges. Today, there are 218 friends' groups nationwide, and that number is growing.

In late February 2002 the NWRA, in cooperation with the Fish and Wildlife Service, sponsored the first National Wildlife Refuge Friends Conference, held in Washington, D.C. More than 270 attendees from 102 refuges and forty-three states, the District of Columbia, and Midway Atoll attended the two-day event. There were formal presentations on the refuge system, techniques for strengthening friends' groups and reaching out to the local communities, and numerous opportunities for friends to informally get to know one another and share stories and strategies for success. One of the main objectives

Reelfoot Lake at the Reelfoot NWR, Tennessee. In August 1997 Reelfoot Lake provided the backdrop for a fugitive chase scene in the 1998 Warner Brothers movie *U.S. Marshals,* starring Tommy Lee Jones, Wesley Snipes, and Robert Downey Jr. The movie crew was very careful to minimize its impact on the refuge lands and even did some restoration work before leaving.

RIGHT: Petroglyphs at the Hart Mountain NWR, Oregon.

of the conference was to create a national, highly trained and coordinated constituency around individual refuges and the refuge system as a whole. And judging by the comments of the participants, many left the meeting energized with a renewed sense of purpose and a deeper understanding of the importance of their role in ensuring the success of the refuge system. Following the conference, the NWRA led 130 conference participants to Capitol Hill to lobby their members of Congress to increase the refuge system's operation and maintenance funding for the coming year by $100 million, a level supported by CARE. Although there have

been lobby days for individual refuges, such as the Arctic NWR, this was the first time that such a geographically diverse group of individuals lobbied collectively for the broader welfare of the refuge system.

To honor refuge volunteers, the NWRA and the National Fish and Wildlife Foundation created an awards program. In 2000, for example, the Friends of the Rydell Refuge Association, located in northwestern Minnesota, was named support group of the year. Although a relatively small and new group, the association was able to achieve great things, including raising more than $260,000 for refuge facilities, creating and

Refuge manager with kids at the Lake Woodruff NWR, Florida.

MIDDLE: Volunteer working with a Boy Scout at the Minnesota Valley NWR, Minnesota.

FAR RIGHT: Apple snail eggs at the Arthur R. Marshall Loxahatchee NWR, Florida.

maintaining 7 miles of refuge trails, and providing educational programs to the public. In 2002 Melissa Owen was selected as volunteer of the year. She had donated more than six thousand hours to the Buenos Aires NWR over six years. During that time she coordinated volunteer efforts, greeted visitors on weekends when the visitor center was closed, expanded the refuge's recycling program, worked with the Friends of Buenos Aires, and initiated the creation of two gardens in the refuge, one for butterflies and the other for native grasses. Upon receiving her award

Owen shared her great enthusiasm for her work and encouraged fellow volunteers to contribute an additional two hours of service each month.

The National Audubon Society has added to the legions of volunteers working at refuges through the Audubon Refuge Keeper (ARK) Program, an outgrowth of the society's earlier Adopt-a-Refuge Program. The goal of the program is to leverage the power of the 518 Audubon chapters to establish "umbrella groups" that will work with refuge staffs to develop educational and public outreach programs on local wildlife. Many Audubon chapters have linked with local refuges under this program and are providing valuable support to the refuge system. One of these is the Atlantic Audubon Society of Atlantic City, New Jersey, which has worked with the nearby Edwin B. Forsythe NWR on a variety of visitor activities, including children's walks, van tours, purple martin house demonstrations, and well-attended birding events.

Many friends' groups, as well as other organizations, support the refuge system by becoming cooperative associations, which are not-for-profit partner corporations authorized by the Fish and Wildlife Service to sell educational materials on refuges, such as books and posters. These materials help to enhance visitors' understanding of and appreciation for conservation efforts and the important role that the refuge system plays in protecting wild places. Each year, the cooperating associations pump hundreds of thousands of dollars back into the refuge system, to be used for various educational, interpretive, biological, and recreational initiatives.

One of the most important tasks facing the refuge system is introducing itself to the public. Even though forty million people per year visit refuges, many more Americans know virtually nothing about the refuge system, which has been called "America's hidden lands." And if they do know something, it is probably due to news coverage of a small number of high-profile stories, such as drilling in the Arctic NWR or the water contamination at the Kesterson NWR. It is not surprising that the refuge system has a low profile when one considers that the agency that houses it, the Fish and Wildlife Service, also suffers to some degree from what former Secretary

of the Interior Cecil Andrus called "a commitment to anonymity." According to Dan Ashe, chief of the National Wildlife Refuge System, one of the more specific reasons for the refuge system's relative anonymity is that during much of its history, the philosophy of the refuge management team was "with very limited exceptions, if we only buy the land, put fences around it, post it, and keep people out of it then we can do good things for wildlife." During that time generating public support was not a major focus for the refuge system.

In the political battle for scarce resources, having a low profile is a distinct disadvantage. A major reason the refuge system has been unable to secure the levels of funding it needs to carry out all of its responsibilities effectively is because it doesn't have a broad-based, powerful constituency fighting on its behalf and making the politicians who hold the purse strings listen. This relative lack of fiscal muscle is manifested not only at the congressional level but also within the Department of the Interior, where the refuge system is one of many programs fighting for scarce budget dollars, and it is often fighting against programs with higher profiles, such as those for endangered species. This is not to say that the refuge system hasn't had strong and passionate supporters in the past. It has and they continue to carry the banner for more funding. But compared with many other government programs with which it has to compete, the refuge system has not been a stellar performer in the battle for bucks. Fortunately, this situation is changing. As Ashe pointed out, "the culture at the Refuge System has been shifting over the last ten years. We realize that we need to let the American public know about the refuge system so that they'll appreciate it, they'll understand it, and they'll support it." By investing in public outreach, partnering with other organizations, fostering its massive volunteer army, and strengthening connections

The centennial logo produced by the Fish and Wildlife Service. *U.S. Fish and Wildlife Service.*

RIGHT: Endangered wood storks with young on two nests at the Harris Neck NWR, Georgia. The birds on the left are perched on a nesting platform built by refuge personnel. The birds on the right have their nest in a natural tree snag.

with all its varied constituencies, the refuge system is, slowly but surely, raising its profile and garnering more financial support. Recent significant increases in refuge system budgets would not have happened had it not been for the focused support of groups such as CARE and the heightened and more diffuse support of the general public.

One way in which the refuge system has successfully connected with the public is through National Wildlife Refuge Week, which is celebrated during the second week of October. Mollie Beattie, the former Fish and Wildlife Service director who established this tradition in 1995, called it "a time for all Americans to learn about and celebrate this magnificent collection of lands we as a people have set aside for wildlife, and for the American spirit." Beattie believed that National Wildlife Refuge Week should be viewed "as a beginning of a renewed awareness and commitment to wildlife conservation, for as Chief Seattle said: 'If all the beasts were gone, man would die from a great loneliness of spirit.'" Each year refuges across the country stage special events during National Wildlife Refuge Week and offer a special invitation to the American public to come visit the refuge system.

Aerial view of the Breton NWR,
Louisiana.

RIGHT: San Lorenzo Canyon at
the Sevilleta NWR, New Mexico.

The centennial celebration, which runs
throughout 2003, offers a golden opportunity for
the refuge system to capture the public's attention, and the National Wildlife Refuge System
Centennial Act of 2000 seeks to capitalize on
that. It established a centennial commission of
notables to oversee special public outreach activities leading up to and during the centennial year,
such as hosting a national conference on the
refuge system. Commission members are almost
as diverse as the refuge system and include
William P. Horn, chairman of the counsel,
Sportsmen's Alliance, and former assistant secretary of interior, Fish and Wildlife and Parks;

Ramona Seligson Bass, board of directors, Fort
Worth Zoo, and director, Texas Wildlife
Campaign; Michael Bean, wildlife program chairman, Environmental Defense; Peter Coors, chairman and chief executive officer, Coors Brewing
Company; Lynn Greenwalt, former director, Fish
and Wildlife Service; Jack Hannah, host of the
television series *Jack Hannah's Animal Adventures;*
Karl Malone, twelve-time NBA All-Star, Utah Jazz
team member, and Olympic gold medallist; John
L. Morris, founder and CEO of Bass Pro Shops
and former chairman of the board, National Fish
and Wildlife Foundation; Kym Murphy, corpo-
rate vice president of environmental policy with

the Walt Disney Company; and Daniel A. Pedrotti, former president of the Boone and Crockett Club and head of Suemaur Exploration, an oil and gas exploration company in Texas.

The centennial act also paved the way for a range of centennial campaign projects. These include turning the Pelican Island NWR into a premier site for conservation education, partnering with the Smithsonian National Zoological Park to create a special exhibit highlighting the refuge system's success with endangered species and migratory waterfowl, producing a commemorative calendar, and building upon existing

efforts to expand and enhance volunteer activities. Another major centennial project is a special exhibit on the refuge system at the National Museum of Natural History, scheduled to run for six months beginning in March 2003 and then possibly going on the road to other locations.

The centennial celebration provides an excellent opportunity to trumpet the past successes of the refuge system. Reflecting on these, Ashe offered the following partial list. "We're providing habitat for millions and millions of migrating waterfowl. We're providing the bridges, the keystones to support the migration of neotropical

Cave salamander at the Logan Cave NWR, Arkansas.

RIGHT: **Northern rough-winged swallow family at the Protection Island NWR, Washington.**

songbirds and shorebirds. We're supporting the recovery of the bald eagle, the peregrine falcon, the whooping crane, and other species that are coming back from the brink of extinction." The centennial also offers a chance to look to the future and set the stage for the next one hundred years of the refuge system. As Kurth stated, "The centennial is intended to have a lasting value, and not just be a big party. We must seize the opportunity that the centennial provides to get visibility for the refuge system, form partnerships that are essential, find champions in Congress, and get us the resources we need to get the job done. This will enable us to take fish and wildlife conservation to a higher level."

The refuge system is constantly changing and evolving, and indeed, that has been one of its greatest strengths. On the eve of its second century, the refuge system is again branching out in new directions. One area of expanded effort is the protection of marine ecosystems. For exam-

ple, in 2001 Congress appropriated almost $10 million to establish the Palmyra Atoll and Kingman Reef NWRs. Palmyra Atoll is U.S. territory roughly 1,000 miles from Hawaii that features a rare rainforest ecosystem, huge numbers of seabirds, and pristine coral reefs. Both Palmyra Atoll and nearby Kingman Reef provide valuable habitat for a dazzling array of marine creatures, including Hawaiian monk seals and several species of sea turtles. Another exciting development is the establishment in late 2001 of America's first international wildlife refuge, located on more than 5,000 acres along the lower Detroit River in Michigan and Canada. The Detroit River International Wildlife Refuge will conserve and restore habitat for sixty-five species of fish and three hundred species of migratory birds. Commenting on this historic event, Bill Hartwig, Midwest regional director of the Fish and Wildlife Service, said,

> This is a great day for the people of Michigan and for the National Wildlife Refuge System. . . . [This refuge] will help link the people of Michigan and other Americans with their natural treasures—the birds, fish and waterfowl that live on and depend on the Lower Detroit River. The refuge also goes a step further by linking Americans and Canadians in a living symbol of both nations' commitment to wildlife conservation.

There is little doubt that in the coming years the refuge system will find other innovative ways to pursue its mission.

15

PROFILES IN BEAUTY

With greater than five hundred NWRs, there is no such thing as a typical refuge. In geography, habitat, and species mix, each one is unique. The following eight profiles are, therefore, only snapshots of the refuge system selected for their beauty and diversity.

BOSQUE DEL APACHE

Every winter, visitors to the Bosque del Apache NWR are treated to one of the most breathtaking wildlife spectacles in the world. As the sun crests the mountain peaks and the first slivers of light illuminate the valley below, tens of thousands of waterfowl rise off the marshes into the sky on their way to feed in the nearby fields. The noise of wings cutting through the air and birds announcing their departure with guttural vocalizations is as loud as a freight train rumbling down the tracks. When dusk settles, the birds fly back to the marshes, where they spend the night resting and waiting for the cycle to begin anew the next day.

Snow geese and sandhill cranes in marsh at the Bosque del Apache NWR.

213

The 57,000-acre Bosque del Apache NWR is located 20 miles south of Socorro, New Mexico, at the northern edge of the Chihuahuan Desert. It straddles the Rio Grande and is bordered by the Chupadera Mountains to the west and the San Pascual Mountains to the east. The refuge was created in 1939 to protect a range of migratory birds and other wildlife, but of particular concern at the time was the status of the sandhill canes. In 1940 only seventeen sandhills wintered on the refuge. Today, up to seventeen thousand do. Each year throngs of people from all over the world come to watch these statuesque, magnificent birds and revel in the natural poetry and beauty of their movement. The late Charles Kuralt, a legendary journalist and ardent supporter of the refuge system, captured the almost mystical quality of these birds when he recalled his initial encounter with them. "I saw them first many Novembers ago," he wrote, "and heard their triumphant trumpet calls, a hundred or more sandhill cranes riding south on a thermal above the Rio Grande Valley, and that day their effortless flight and their brassy music got into my soul."

Sandhill cranes are the stars of the Bosque del Apache NWR, but they share the stage with numerous species—more than 350 in the avian class alone. Like the sandhills, snow geese were a rare sight in the early years of the refuge, with only thirty individuals wintering there in 1939. Today, that number is thirty thousand. Other feathered residents of the refuge include bald eagles, American kestrels, Gambel's quail, northern shovelers, red-tailed hawks, white-crowned sparrows, and great horned owls. Sharing the landscape with the birds are mule deer, coyotes, black-tailed jackrabbits, occult little brown bats, and prairie rattlesnakes, among other species.

The Bosque del Apache NWR has a long history of human habitation. More than seven hundred years ago, the Piro Indians settled in the valley to take advantage of its rich soils and abundant plant and animal life. By the late 1500s when

Greater sandhill crane at the Bosque del Apache NWR.

MIDDLE: Wetland habitat and reflections at the Bosque del Apache NWR.

FAR RIGHT: Sandhill crane in flight at the Bosque del Apache NWR.

Spanish colonists established El Camino Real (the royal road), a 1,200-mile trade route between Mexico City and Santa Fe, they found the Piros still living in the area. In the years that followed, a few Spanish settlers located along the trade route, and today visitors to the refuge can see remnants of the Piro and El Camino Real occupation within the refuge's borders. The Apache people also frequently camped in the bottomland forest that grew along the banks of the river, and it is to that historical fact that the refuge owes its name—Bosque del Apache, or "woods of the Apache." In the mid-1800s, Anglos joined the rich cultural mix of the area.

Throughout this history the natural cycle of river flooding replenished the valley lands with nutrients and provided valuable, albeit ephemeral, aquatic habitat that sustained healthy and diverse wildlife populations. But when in the early twentieth century the Rio Grande was tamed with dams, canals, and ditches to provide a stable source of water for farm irrigation and other human needs, the restorative floods became a memory, and the natural system that had been built upon the reliability of periodic drenching withered away. The land that the Fish and Wildlife Service was given with the creation of the Bosque del Apache NWR was therefore, like so much new refuge land, severely degraded and in need of extensive management to make it productive wildlife habitat.

Refuge staff, volunteers, and others have worked hard to make the Bosque del Apache NWR the success it is today. The centerpiece of

Autumn elk herd gathered in Missouri River bottomland at the Charles M. Russell NWR.

those efforts and the heart of the refuge is a 7,000-acre floodplain where the waters of the Rio Grande are diverted to create extensive wetlands. The practice of moist soil management manipulates the levels of the wetlands to ensure a range of habitat conditions. After being tilled or burned, dry impoundments are flooded, allowing wetland plants to grow. When a wetland reaches maturity and its productivity falters, it is drained, and the cycle begins anew. In this way the vitality and diversity of the habitat are maintained.

Crops are planted on refuge lands to ensure that wintering waterfowl have enough food to eat. Local farmers grow corn and alfalfa, harvesting the alfalfa and leaving the corn behind for the birds. Refuge staff add to the amount of forage by growing corn, winter wheat, clover, and native plants. Refuge workers are also working to restore the cottonwood and willow bosques that once lined the river's edge. To do this, the first task is getting rid of the salt cedar, or tamarisk, a species introduced for beauty and erosion control that has engulfed large areas of the refuge and, unfortunately, provides few benefits to wildlife. Once the salt cedar is cleared, cottonwoods, willows, and shrubs are planted.

The Friends of Bosque del Apache NWR play a major role in the life of the refuge. In addition to hosting the annual Festival of the Cranes, which is attended by well over ten thousand people from all over the world, the friends produce a newspaper, the *Bosque del Apache Habitat!* They also run an extensive nature store to raise money for refuge projects and volunteer numerous hours on various refuge projects.

CHARLES M. RUSSELL

For sixteen days in May 1805, Meriwether Lewis and William Clark led the Corps of Discovery up the Missouri River through an area that is

now part of the 1.1-million-acre Charles M. Russell NWR, located in northeastern Montana. Journal entries penned by members of the corps during this relatively brief segment of their four-year journey through the uncharted West depict a rugged, untamed landscape abundant in wildlife and sublime beauty. Much of the land remains that way today. If one's goal were to see what the Old West looked like when it was still a mystery to most Americans, there is hardly a better place to do so than the Charles M. Russell NWR. It is a living monument to an important part of the natural heritage of the United States.

The Charles M. Russell NWR is the second-largest refuge in the lower forty-eight (after the Desert NWR) and is the roughly the size of Delaware. It spans 125 miles as the crow flies and completely engulfs the enormous Fort Peck Reservoir and the UL Bend NWR. The labyrinthine landscape of the Charles M. Russell NWR embraces cliffs, canyons, arroyos, mesas, cottonwood and willow bottomlands, coulees, Douglas fir and ponderosa pine woodlands, prairie grasslands, and windswept ridges atop deeply furrowed hills. The refuge straddles the mighty Missouri River, which is fed by other rivers and numerous creeks that give rise to the area's moniker the Missouri Breaks.

Herds of elk, pronghorn antelope, and bighorn sheep roam the refuge, alongside coyotes, bobcats, badgers, mink, and mule and white-tailed deer. Gone are the grizzly bears, bison, and wolves, and gone forever not only from this area but from the face of the earth are the majestic Audubon sheep, the last of which was killed in 1916. More than 230 species of birds have been recorded at the refuge, including double-crested cormorants, prairie falcons, Clark's nutcrackers, pinyon jays, semipalmated plovers, and black-capped chickadees. Each spring, sharp-tailed grouse congregate on their dancing grounds, or "leks," to perform their dramatic courtship rituals in which the males arch their wings, stomp their feet, rush to and fro, twist about, and make loud rattling noises by shaking their feathers, all in an effort to outperform each other in the pursuit of the perfect mate. Under the surface of the broad and swift Missouri River swim sturgeons, catfish, sticklebacks, drums, and gars. But the oddest species of all is the paddlefish, a prehistoric, filter-feeding holdover that has no bones, just cartilage, and can grow to more than 100 pounds. The fish's name comes from its large paddle-shaped snout, the purpose of which is unknown.

A small population of black-footed ferrets, one of the most endangered mammals in the world, lives within the UL Bend NWR and is managed by the staff at the Charles M. Russell NWR. Ferrets not only live in the underground burrow systems prairie dogs create and maintain but also depend entirely on the prairie dogs for their diet. Therefore, it was no surprise that as the prairie dog population was decimated during the early to mid–twentieth century due to a combination of habitat destruction, rodent-eradication programs, and disease, the population of ferrets also sank, so much so that by the 1970s biologists surmised that the black-footed ferret was extinct, or nearly so. A remnant population of ferrets was found in Wyoming in 1981, but disease threatened it with extinction. The last eighteen ferrets in the world were

caught in 1986 to protect them and initiate a captive-breeding program. The Black-Footed Ferret Recovery Plan's goal is to establish at least ten self-sustaining ferret populations with a minimum of 1,500 ferrets in the wild by 2010. Captive-reared ferrets were released at the UL Bend NWR between 1994 and 1999, and nearly two hundred wild-born kits have been produced there. There are currently twenty to twenty-five ferrets at the refuge.

During its sojourn in the area, the Corps of Discovery was impressed by the land and its animals. On May 9, 1805, Lewis wrote of seeing "the most extraordinary river that I ever beheld." It contained not "a single drop of running water," but instead was completely dry and a half-mile wide. He called it the "Big dry river," a name it still has today. In the same entry he added, "we saw a great quantity of game today particularly of Elk and Buffaloe, the latter are now so gentle that

Painting by Charles M. Russell, titled *Buccaroos from the N-N Outfit in the Big Dry in Montana.* This image appeared as part of a folio of four Russell prints under the title "Some Incidents of Western Life" in the February 1905 issue of *Scribner's Magazine. Library of Congress.*

RIGHT: Portrait of Charles M. Russell in western attire, taken sometime between 1880 and 1910. *Library of Congress.*

the men frequently throw sticks and stones at them in order to drive them out of the way." Two days later, Lewis wrote of an encounter with a grizzly bear.

> About 5 P.M. my attention was struck by one of the party running at a distance towards us and making signs and hollowing as if in distress, . . . I now found that it was Bratton . . . at length he informed me . . . below us he had shot a brown bear which immediately turned on him and pursued him a considerable distance but he had wounded it so badly that it could not overtake him; . . . it was a monstrous beast, not quite so large as that we killed a few days past but in all other rispects much the same . . . we now found that Bratton had shot him through the center of the lungs, notwithstanding which he had pursued him near half a mile and had returned more than double that distance and with his tallons had prepared himself a bed in the earth of about 2 feet deep and five long and was perfectly alive when we

found him which could not have been less than 2 hours after he received the wound; these bear being so hard to die reather intimedates us all; I must confess that I do not like the gentlemen and had reather fight two Indians than one bear.

On the same day as the bear attack, one of the corpsmen, John Ordway, noted that "these hill[s] bair the first pine we have Seen on this River. the country back from the River is broken, but the Soil verry rich and good. the River bottoms are Smoth and level thinly covred with cotton wood timber, and filled with all most all kinds of Game."

In the decades after Lewis and Clark finished their travels through the Northwest and reported back to Thomas Jefferson, others came to the region. There were the trappers and market hunters, whose determined efforts managed to strip much of the landscape of small fur-bearing animals and large game such as the bison. In 1859 the first steam-powered riverboat navigated up the Missouri on its way to Fort Benton through what is now the Charles M. Russell NWR. This form of travel continued until it was made obsolete in the late 1880s by the tracks and freight cars of the Great Northern and Pacific Railroads. After steamboats began plying the Missouri and before the railroad opened the Northwest, stockmen moved into the area so that their herds of cattle and other livestock could feed on Montana's prairie grasses. Big ranches dotted the countryside and served as magnets for cattle rustlers and horse thieves. Ranchers didn't take kindly to having their animals taken, and in perhaps the area's most famous case of vigilante justice, Granville Stuart, operator of the DHS ranch, led a group of local stockmen to take care of a large horse-thieving ring once and for all. In short order they hung four of the thieves and then killed five more in a gun battle. Seven of the thieves, though, managed to escape. Five of them were soon captured by soldiers in eastern Montana and turned over to Stuart's gang, who quickly lived up to the nickname "Stuart's Stranglers" and hung the men from cottonwood trees down by the Musselshell River near where it feeds into the Missouri. Stuart's Stranglers were roundly condemned, but that was the last of organized horse rustling in the Missouri Breaks, and Stuart later became the first president of the Montana Stockgrowers Association. The area's connection to livestock remains strong. Today, more than seven thousand domestic cattle graze on land that lies within the refuge's boundaries.

In 1935 naturalist and Bureau of Biological Survey employee Olaus Murie was asked to do a biological study of the area, and he, like Lewis and Clark, was impressed. "This region as a whole is extremely picturesque. . . . The very landscape is appealing. A camp out in the badlands, with the jumble of carved and stratified buttes perhaps mellowed by the setting sun or set off by cloud formations at dawn, leaves nothing to be desired. . . . Simplicity on a grand scale is the keynote of this whole outdoor picture." Using Murie's report for support, President Franklin Delano Roosevelt signed an order creating the Fort Peck Game Range. In 1963 the range was renamed in honor of the famed western artist Charles M. Russell, and then in 1976 it was officially made a national wildlife refuge.

Russell was born in 1864 in St. Louis, Missouri. Just shy of his sixteenth birthday he pursued his dream of going west, ultimately settling in the Montana Territory, his home for the rest of his life. A self-taught painter, Russell loved the West, and that showed in his paintings and bronze sculptures, which presented an unvarnished and unsentimental view of life on the range for Native Americans, fur traders, cowboys, and wildlife. For inspiration he drew, in part, on his early years as a wrangler and was often referred to as "America's cowboy artist." His legacy of four thousand works of art captures the essence of the American West and serves as a powerful visual link to this bygone era. Russell was also a conservationist at heart who, for example, worried about the impact that the widespread plowing of grasslands would have on the balance of nature. The Charles M. Russell NWR brilliantly reflects the passions of the complex man for which it is named.

Each year, roughly sixty thousand people visit the refuge, which includes large areas of wilderness, to pursue a wide range of activities, including hiking, photography, boating, fishing, and hunting. Another activity, pursued by a select few trained and authorized paleontologists, is dinosaur hunting. The Charles M. Russell NWR has been the site of many significant dinosaur discoveries, including the largest *Tyrannosaurus rex* ever found. In recent years the remains of seven more of these colossal beasts from the distant past have been uncovered on the refuge.

CHINCOTEAGUE

On their annual migrations north and south, millions of waterfowl travel along the Atlantic flyway, which for much of its length is a relatively narrow band that hugs the eastern seaboard of the United States. There are many NWRs that aid the birds in their journeys, and one of the most important is the Chincoteague NWR, located on a series of barrier islands off the coasts of Virginia and Maryland. When Rachel Carson wrote about the Chincoteague NWR in the first of the Fish and Wildlife Service's Conservation in Action series, her simple words captured why the refuge was created in 1943. "If we are to preserve the remaining waterfowl, and the sports and recreation which depend on them," she said, "we must set apart for the birds refuges like Chincoteague, where they may find these simple and necessary creature comforts: food, rest, security." Although the refuge's goals have since expanded to include the protection of a wide range of wildlife, as well as the provision of wildlife-dependent education and recreation, the Chincoteague NWR is still largely about the birds.

The Chincoteague NWR encompasses more than 14,000 acres of beach, dune, marsh, and forest habitat, primarily on the southern end of Assateague Island. The vast majority of the refuge is in Virginia, with a small shoot of less than 500 acres reaching into Maryland. In addition the refuge boundary extends south to encompass all or part of the following barrier islands: Assawoman, Metompkin, and Cedar.

The refuge's bird list numbers over 325. Migratory waterfowl, of course, are well represented. Canada geese, scaup, tundra swans, pintails, teal, buffleheads, American wigeons (baldplates), red-breasted mergansers, snow geese, and American brant all make an appearance or remain for an extended engagement during various times of the year. One can also see a great variety of shorebirds, raptors, wading birds, and songbirds, including semipalmated sandpipers, ruddy turnstones, ospreys, northern harriers, yellow-crowned night herons, great egrets, indigo buntings, and cedar waxwings. Lucky birders might glimpse a swift and beautiful peregrine falcon diving or "stooping" toward an unsuspecting bird at speeds of more than 200 miles per hour and then killing it with a sharp blow. And the Chincoteague NWR lays claim to more pairs of the Atlantic Coast population of threatened piping plovers than any other refuge. To make the refuge more inviting to migratory birds, refuge staff constructed 2,600 acres of fresh- and brackish-water impoundments, and they manage woodlands where the birds can rest and feed.

The birds share the refuge with other animals, including northern diamondback terrapins, eastern hognose snakes, fowler's toads, meadow jumping mice, river otters, and Sika elks, an Asian species first introduced to Assateague Island in the 1920s. Threatened Atlantic loggerhead turtles and endangered Delmarva fox squirrels are also present, and one can spy bottlenose dolphins from the beach. A properly timed walk on one of the refuge's trails will reveal blooming meadow beauties, crested yellow orchids, rose mallow, and evening primrose.

Moonrise over saltwater marsh at
the Chincoteague NWR.

Wild ponies at the Chincoteague NWR. The number 4 on the side of one of the ponies is a brand that the Chincoteague Volunteer Fire Department placed there to keep track of the herd. Today, ponies are individually tracked through computer chips implanted in the ponies' lips. *Greg Knadle and the U.S. Fish and Wildlife Service.*

Well-known inhabitants of the Chincoteague NWR are the wild ponies. The ponies' leap to international fame was spurred by Marguerite Henry's classic children's book *Misty of Chincoteague,* written in 1947, in which two children fall in love with, buy, and raise a pony named Misty, the foal of the mysterious Phantom. There are 150 adult ponies that are owned by the Chincoteague Volunteer Fire Department and are allowed to graze on the refuge under a special permit. Another, similar-sized herd lives on the Maryland side of Assateague Island and is managed by the National Park Service. Nobody is sure where the ponies came from, but there are plenty

of theories. Some argue that the first ponies swam ashore from a shipwrecked Spanish galleon. Others think the ponies are descended from horses that plundering pirates put ashore. It is most likely, however, that the ponies' ancestors are domestic horses whose owners had them graze in the area during colonial times to avoid taxes on the mainland.

Each year, at the end of July, thousands of people descend on Chincoteague Island to watch the pony penning and auction. The ponies, rounded up by saltwater cowboys, swim across the narrowest part of Assateague Channel at slack tide. The ponies are placed in pens, and during the ensuing

Birdwatchers observing snow geese at the Chincoteague NWR. Bird watching is a popular activity at hundreds of NWRs. The American Bird Conservancy recently produced a list of the 546 globally most significant bird areas in the United States. Roughly one-third of those listed are NWRs, including Chincoteague.

auction many of the foals and some of the yearlings are sold to raise money for the Chincoteague Volunteer Fire Department. Although penning the wild ponies is a local tradition that dates back to the 1600s, its modern incarnation began in 1924, when the townspeople decided to sell ponies as a way of financing the purchase of new fire equipment. In the early days ponies went for around $20. Today, the average is close to one hundred times that. In 2000 the auction raised more than $173,000, and one horse went for an impressive $7,500. Selling the ponies not only helps the fire department protect the people of Chincoteague but also keeps the numbers of ponies below the maximum number of 150 that the Fish and Wildlife Service has determined is the most that the refuge can support.

The Chincoteague NWR gets roughly 1.5 million visitors per year. Unfortunately, the 1974-vintage visitor center that greets these people is a diminutive 1,156-square-foot structure with a small room where visitors can view videos. For many years the refuge staff have dreamed of a larger visitor center, and in 2003 their dreams will come true with the dedication of the Herbert H. Bateman Educational and Administrative Center, replete with offices,

exhibits, a sales outlet, a Windows to the Wild observation area, and an auditorium that can seat 125. This addition will be especially welcomed by the thousands of schoolchildren who visit the refuge annually to participate in the wide variety and large number of educational and interpretive programs run by refuge staff.

Refuge staff receive plenty of support from the Chincoteague Refuge Volunteers and the local friends group, the Chincoteague Natural History Association, which provides services ranging from creating educational materials and hosting International Migratory Bird Day to funding student interns and running junior birder programs. In 2000 two of the Chincoteague refuge volunteers, Paul and Ann Smith, a husband-wife team, were named volunteers of the year by the National Wildlife Refuge Association and the National Fish and Wildlife Foundation. The Smiths have contributed thousands of hours to helping a wide range of the refuge's programs. They focus special attention on shorebirds, providing the Fish and Wildlife Service with bird counts that have been used by it and other organizations that monitor the health of shorebird populations. To raise money for the new visitor center, the

the southern end of San Francisco Bay, this 26,000-acre refuge spans twelve cities and three counties and is within easy driving distance of more than eight million people. If it weren't for the efforts of a small but dedicated group of local citizens, this refuge would never have been created, and one of the last remnants of San Francisco Bay's wild heritage would have been lost to development.

When the first Spanish explorers set eyes on the San Francisco Bay in the late 1700s, the beauty of the land and its wildlife amazed them. Sea captains recorded wondrous scenes in their logs. "There is not any country in the world," wrote Captain Compte de la Perouse, "which more abounds in fish and game of every description." A rifle shot was said to cause huge numbers of waterfowl and shorebirds to rise "in a dense cloud with a noise like that of a hurricane." Some of the early settlers were not so enamored with their wilder neighbors. One missionary referred to the area's elk as "monsters with tremendous horns," while another looked upon the enormous and plentiful grizzly bears and pronounced them "horrible, fierce, large, and fat."

Not long after the Spanish established the first bay-area mission in 1776, cattle ranchers, fur traders, and others determined to reap profit from the land began plying their trades and eroding the region's natural capital. The discovery of gold in 1848 transformed the region with astonishing rapidity. In two years the population of San Francisco exploded from four hundred to twenty-five thousand. Hydraulic mining operations scoured entire hillsides with high-pressured blasts of water, sending vast rivers of silt into streams and rivers that fed into the bay, where the silt settled, raising the bottom by as much as 3 feet, altering circulation patterns, and creating new marshlands. In 1854 Captain John Johnson launched the first commercial salt-harvesting

Chincoteague Natural History Association has been selling stuffed TR bears and TR baby bears, which are not only named after the presidential founder of the refuge system but also look a little like President Theodore Roosevelt, complete with a bushy mustache and a Rough Rider hat.

DON EDWARDS SAN FRANCISCO BAY

The Don Edwards San Francisco Bay NWR is a wildlife oasis in the midst of one of the most populated urban areas in the nation. Sitting at

operation in the bay, a process that converts salt marshes into salt ponds and uses the energy of the sun to evaporate the water, leaving a crusty layer of salt behind. Others followed in Johnson's footsteps, including the Leslie Salt Company, which in 1936 purchased 40,000 acres of marshlands and salt ponds for salt production. And throughout the 1800s and up through the mid-1900s, cities and towns formed and grew along the edges of the bay, replacing the natural environment with fill and human structures and polluting the bay with sewage and industrial waste.

In 1960 a study by the U.S. Corps of Engineers concluded that at the current rate of development the bay would be a river by 2010. To help avert this fate, the Save San Francisco Bay Association formed in 1961 with the main goals of preventing further filling and increasing public access to the shoreline. "Bay or River?" was the association's rallying cry. Another group that formed around this time was the South San Francisco Baylands Planning, Conservation, and National Wildlife Refuge Committee. When this group approached the federal government with

LEFT: Dunes and wetlands at the Chincoteague NWR.

Black-necked stilts wade in shallow waters within sight of industrial development at the Don Edwards San Francisco Bay NWR.

Biking tour through the wetlands at the Don Edwards San Francisco Bay NWR.

RIGHT: Visitor center at the Don Edwards San Francisco Bay NWR.

the idea of establishing a refuge in the bay, the Fish and Wildlife Service expressed little interest. Instead of giving up on the idea, the committee enlisted the help of local politicians, including Congressman Don Edwards, went to the nation's capitol with its appeal, and achieved success. In 1972 President Richard Nixon signed the legislation to create the refuge, and in 1974 the San Francisco Bay NWR officially came into existence. And it was not a moment too soon, for at the time it was estimated that upwards of 85 percent of the bay's wetlands had been lost to development. In 1995 the refuge was renamed to honor Edwards, who had since retired, for his

longstanding and active support of the refuge.

The legislation establishing the refuge authorized the purchase of 23,000 acres. By the early 1980s it became apparent that this was not sufficient to adequately protect the wildlife in the area. Once again, committed citizens mobilized their forces. The Citizen's Committee to Complete the Refuge, working with Edwards and others, lobbied Congress to expand the ultimate size of the refuge, and in 1988 those efforts paid off when legislation authorized the refuge to grow to 43,000 acres. Achieving that goal moved one step closer to realization when Cargill Corporation offered to sell 19,000 acres of its salt ponds, which span 20 miles of shoreline and adjoin the refuge, to the government for roughly $300 million. Realizing that coming up with such a huge sum would be close to impossible, Senator Diane Feinstein of California proposed a compromise in July of 2001 in which 12,000 acres would be purchased for $100 million. Finding the money has been difficult. To date, California has put up $25 million for the purchase, and Congress another $8 million. When Secretary of the Interior Gale Norton visited the Don Edwards San Francisco Bay NWR in January 2002, she voiced approval for the plan, saying, "It's no secret that we think that would be a wonderful addition to the refuge system." But Norton did not indicate that the administration was willing to provide any funds to help secure the land. Still, the proponents of the plan are guardedly optimistic that the money will be found through a combination of public and private sources.

The Don Edwards San Francisco Bay NWR is one of the most important links in the Pacific flyway, and millions of waterfowl, shorebirds, and songbirds use it as a temporary refueling point or a place to stay during their annual migrations. More than 250 species of birds can be found on the refuge during the year, including barn swallows, orange-crowned warblers, canvasbacks, pintails, least sandpipers, and avocets. Other animal and plant species on view include tiger salamanders, cordgrass, pickleweed, harbor seals, gray foxes, jackrabbits, swallow-tail butterflies, and many types of mollusks. The Don Edwards San Francisco Bay NWR also has a complement of endangered and threatened species, including the California clapper rail, the western snowy plover, and the salt marsh harvest mouse. Habitats offered by the refuge range from mudflats, salt ponds, and salt marshes to upland areas and ephemeral vernal pools that

can be dry for up to eight months out of the year yet are key to the survival of species such as the vernal pool tadpole shrimp and the Contra Costa goldfields.

One of the most important goals of the Don Edwards San Francisco Bay NWR is educating the public about the importance of wildlife, and it boasts the most active educational program in the refuge system. Many of the more than four hundred thousand annual visitors take self-guided and informative hikes through the refuge and participate in educational activities offered by refuge staff and volunteers, such as the Twilight Marsh Walk and a Geological Trip through Time. There is a special emphasis on young people, the ones who will inherit public lands and be making the conservation policy

decisions of the future. The environmental education center and the visitor center provide programs for ten thousand schoolchildren, teachers, and parents each year, including Wetland Round-Up and Trekking the Refuge field trips, providing kids with a hands-on opportunity to experience nature and understand the importance of the natural rhythms of the bay. Other activities for

Abandoned building in
Drawbridge, a ghost town
located within the Don Edwards
San Francisco Bay NWR.

RIGHT: Snowy egret in breeding
plumage at the J. N. "Ding"
Darling NWR.

children include Kid's Day at the Refuge and
Junior Naturalist's Summer Day Camp.

The Don Edwards San Francisco Bay NWR
has one of the largest volunteer programs in the
refuge system. For every paid hour of work at
the refuge, volunteers provide an equal amount.
These incredibly effective force multipliers do
everything from removing tons of invasive plants
and monitoring species to leading tours and
operating the visitor center. Through special
projects, volunteers assist species in need of help.
For example, volunteers build mesh wire enclo-
sures around the nests of snowy plovers to help
this endangered species to breed undisturbed.

On October 18, 1997, the Don Edwards San
Francisco Bay NWR celebrated its silver anniversary. It also celebrated Florence and Philip

LaRiviere, longtime champions of the refuge
who helped to get it established and who continue to volunteer their time and energy to complete the refuge and ensure that it remains
vibrant. On that day the restored salt marsh at
the entrance to the refuge was renamed the
LaRiviere Marsh. It was a particularly fitting
tribute for a refuge where citizen activists and
volunteers have made such a difference.

J. N. "DING" DARLING

Darling is a giant in the history of conservation,
best known for his stint in Washington, D.C., as
the dynamic head of the Bureau of Biological
Survey, for which he roused the refuge system
out of its relative torpor and initiated arguably
the most exciting period of growth in its history.

He also helped found the venerable National Wildlife Federation, and through many of his brilliant political cartoons, he captured the plight of the nation's wildlife and natural resources with compelling honesty. But Darling's good works in conservation were hardly limited to events taking place on the national stage. In the early 1940s Darling learned that developers were planning to buy 2,200 acres of mangrove wetlands on Sanibel Island, located just off the coast of Fort Meyers on the Gulf coast of Florida; the price, $0.50 per acre. Sanibel, next to Captiva Island, where Darling wintered, was close to his heart, and he quickly led a successful effort to get the Fish and Wildlife Service to lease the threatened lands, thereby creating the Sanibel NWR in 1945. Soon after Darling died in 1962, his many friends and admirers, who had been inspired by his dedication to conservation, launched the J. N. "Ding" Darling Foundation, which immediately went to work to transfer the refuge's leased lands to federal ownership, thereby protecting them from potential development. By 1967 the transfer was complete, and the refuge was renamed the J. N. "Ding" Darling NWR; a well-deserved tribute to a man whose name is so intimately intertwined with the history of this refuge and the entire refuge system.

Sanibel Island is a mecca for tourism. People come from all over the world to experience the beauty of this subtropical paradise. Here they can perform the famous "Sanibel stoop" as they lean down to scoop up the beautiful seashells that litter the white beaches. The 6,400-acre J. N. "Ding" Darling NWR is also a major destination. It draws nearly one million visitors annually, many of whom take advantage of the 4-mile wildlife drive that loops through the heart of a mangrove forest where the sights and sounds of the refuge are on display. Within the refuge's borders there

are black and red mangroves, the last of which is the most common and has been called "the tree that walks" for its tangled, stiltlike roots. Other habitats include tropical hardwood hammocks, interior freshwater marshes, and beach dunes. Wildlife is abundant throughout. The refuge is known as one of the best birding areas in the nation. On an average day birders can expect to see 75 of the more than 230 species in the area. Among these are anhingas, roseate spoonbills, yellow-crowned night-herons, white ibises, ruddy turnstones, and black skimmers. The refuge also offers protection to a wide array of threatened and endangered species, including the eastern indigo snakes, Atlantic loggerhead turtles, wood storks, and bald eagles.

But the species that is most popular with visitors and that elicits the most universal awe is the threatened American alligator, and there are plenty of them to watch. These ancient reptiles that have been around since the time of the dinosaurs grow to lengths of 15 feet and have powerful jaws, studded with rows of pearly white pointed teeth. They can be seen sunning themselves on land or swimming lazily

on the surface of the water. Alligators can be extremely dangerous, and visitors are warned to keep their distance. The refuge also lays claim to a single female endangered American crocodile, the northernmost individual of this species known to exist. In recent years she has deposited eggs at nesting sites, but without males in the area the eggs have all been infertile.

Much of the refuge's success is due to the work of dedicated volunteers. In 1982, when the first visitor center opened, it was immediately swamped with thousands of people, more than the refuge staff could handle. So the staff turned to the Sanibel-Captiva Audubon Society for help, and it, in turn, launched the "Ding" Darling Wildlife Society, a nonprofit cooperat-

ing association that has as its mission making available refuge-related educational materials and providing materials or donations of money that can be used to further refuge projects and goals. The society, which is the largest refuge cooperating association in the country, is a stunning success. Its many projects include raising money for brochures and species checklists, funding volunteer work, cosponsoring the "Ding" Darling Birthday and Federal Duck Stamp Celebration, and acting as an intermediary in the purchase of additional land for the refuge. The society has earned many national

honors, including being named the 1999 friends' group of the year, an award that cited the society's "exceptional innovation and excellence in advancing the mission of the Refuge System, and its outstanding leadership as a voice of the community and as an advocate for the protection, conservation, and enhancement of local refuges and the National Wildlife Refuge System overall."

The society's most impressive project to date is the "Ding" Darling Education Center, which opened in the fall of 2001 and was more than seven years in the making. The breathtaking $3 million facility was funded entirely by private donations. A walk through the 4,000-square-foot exhibit hall is a journey of discovery. The studio where Darling penned his famous cartoons is recreated, and it includes his original drawing board. Another exhibit shows how estuarine mangrove habitat changes hour by hour throughout the day. An area called Connections tells of the close relationships between people and natural resources, upstream and downstream, uplands to lowlands, and refuge to refuge. Nearby, lifelike models of the red mangroves illustrate how this habitat sustains animals and plants. Rookery Island describes the importance of rookeries as breeding grounds for colonial nesting birds. Elsewhere in the center, where a large taxidermy crocodile stands guard, the heroes of the Fish and Wildlife Service are given their due and the Fish and Wildlife Service's mission is explained. Younger visitors can go to the Discovery Room, where they can touch manatee and sea turtle bones and "build a bird" using Velcro body parts. Finally, a room overlooking the back of the center offers tips on spotting avian species, displays pictures of the most common ones found in the refuge, and even has a few binoculars for trying out new skills.

LEFT: Endangered wood stork at the J. N. "Ding" Darling NWR.

MIDDLE: Endangered American crocodile at the J. N. "Ding" Darling NWR. *David Gilliam and the U.S. Fish and Wildlife Service.*

RIGHT: Roseate spoonbills at the J. N. "Ding" Darling NWR.

Native prairie at the Neal Smith NWR.

RIGHT: Sunrise through native prairie grasses at the Neal Smith NWR.

NEAL SMITH

One hundred and fifty years ago, tallgrass prairie and savanna covered the Iowan landscape. Downy gentian, prairie larkspur, lead plant, creamy indigo, compass plant, Indian paintbrush, starry campion, hairy wild licorice, and other prairie and savanna plants carpeted the countryside in a profusion of textures and range of colors worthy of an artist's palette. Today, less than one-tenth of 1 percent of this habitat remains. The Neal Smith NWR, located 20 miles east of Des Moines, Iowa, is on a mission to bring pieces of the prairie and savanna back and restore an important part of the state's natural heritage.

What happened in Iowa is not unique. Before white settlers came to the area, much of the Midwest was prairie and savanna. But most settlers viewed the prairie and savanna not as things of beauty but as hindrances to progress. In relatively short order vast stretches of the natural landscape were cut down, dug up, and plowed under to make way for farming, roads, railroads, cities, and towns. The destruction of the prairie and savanna continued to the point that now all that are left of these oceans of grass and wildflowers are small degraded remnants scattered through the heartland like islands in a vast agricultural sea.

In the late 1980s support grew for establishing a prairie and savanna restoration project in Iowa, and in 1990, Congress approved the project and authorized the creation of an 8,654-acre refuge to carry it out. Originally called the Walnut Creek NWR, its name was changed in 1995 to the Neal Smith NWR to honor the Iowa congressman who had played a pivotal role in its creation. The project really took off in 1991 when Iowa Light and Power scrapped its plans to build a nuclear power plant outside of Des Moines and put the land for the proposed site up for sale. The Fish and Wildlife Service quickly purchased 3,662 acres as the nucleus for the refuge. Today, the refuge is just over 5,000 acres.

At its inception the refuge was primarily made up of land that had been used to raise cattle, corn, and soybeans. It was up to the restoration team of refuge staff and a small army of volunteers to bring back the prairie and savanna that had existed on this spot before settlement. There were no roadmaps for the team to follow. This restoration project is a prototype, the first of its kind. Never before had a conservation entity tried to rebuild tallgrass prairie and savanna on former agricultural land. To be as true to history as possible, the restoration team studied General Land Office Surveys and notes for the area from the 1840s. The team also looked at old soil maps, gathered local anecdotal information, and investigated nearby prairie remnants, including a few on the refuge's property, for clues to species composition.

Once the team determined what the prairie should look like, it began restoring the natural landscape. Team members scoured the countryside collecting and purchasing seeds, 10 pounds of which are required to plant a single acre. On-site greenhouses were used to sprout seedlings and start garden plots, and seeds harvested from these plots have served as a source for adding diversity to the plantings. When the team learned that prairie or savanna remnants were slated for destruction, they offered to dig up the plants and transfer them to the refuge.

Plant species are only part of the story. Animals and insects traditionally associated with prairie and savanna habitats also need to be

Bison next to big bluestem grass at the Neal Smith NWR. There was a time when bison and elk were plentiful on the prairie of Iowa and other midwestern states. But by the early nineteenth century these noble animals were already becoming a memory.

In 1827 Chief Sabonee of the Potawatomi Indians, which were then located in parts of Michigan, Wisconsin, Indiana, and Illinois, recalled the changes he had seen.

In my youthful days, I have seen large herds of buffalo on these prairies, and elk were found in every grove, but they are here no more, having gone towards the setting sun. For hundreds of miles no white man lived, but now trading posts and settlers are found here and there throughout the country, and in a few years the smoke from their cabins will be seen to ascend from every grove, and the prairie covered with their cornfields.

restored. While the refuge is too small to rein-troduce top-level predators like wolves, many other animals are making a comeback. For example, bison and elk have been reintroduced, and the refuge staff is hoping one day soon to have a resident population of prairie chickens. Regal fritillary butterflies, a very rare endemic prairie species, are also making a return. Once researchers learned that the larvae of these but-terflies probably require prairie violets to feed on, the restoration team transplanted more than one thousand potted violet plants throughout the refuge. And the team has recently begun introducing gravid (pregnant) butterflies. The results of this first-of-its-kind experiment will enable the restoration team to better understand and engineer the species reintroduction process.

Another piece of the restoration puzzle is recreating the physical environment upon which all of the prairie and savanna species depend. There are ongoing efforts to restore local hydrologic and soil conditions. And because the prairie and savanna are fire-dependent ecosystems, fire has once again been introduced to the landscape through prescribed burns to invigorate plantings and increase the quality of the habitat.

The restoration efforts, which continue today, have been very successful and constitute the largest tallgrass prairie and savanna ecosystem reconstruction in the United States. To date, 2,200 acres have been planted to prairie, and more than 1,000 acres of prairie and savanna remnants that are scattered throughout the refuge are gradually being connected via annual native plantings. The restoration effort at the Neal Smith NWR is a critical part of ensuring that these globally endangered ecosystems survive. And the refuge's work also feeds into and supports similar work being done beyond the refuge's borders, on both public and private lands large and small.

The focal point of the refuge is the Neal Smith Prairie Learning Center, established in 1997. This beautiful 40,000-square-foot building, with a 13,000-square-foot exhibit hall, a theater, and labs, is called "earth-connected" because it is sandwiched between two hills and partly buried in the soil. As a result, the building is somewhat protected from the extremes of the weather, and it also benefits from the earth's relatively constant temperature, which provides warmth in the winter and cooling in the summer. Other green touches include energy-efficient windows and a sewage system that discharges to a septic field and a wetland constructed on-site, rather than to a local sewage treatment plant. Refuge staff and volunteers run an innovative environmental education program that includes guided hikes, seed collection outings, and Stewardship Saturdays, during which visitors can learn, firsthand, what it means to reconstruct a natural landscape. The Friends of the Prairie Learning Center has played a big role in the refuge's success. Some of the group's many activities are publishing the *Prairie Wind* newsletter, maintaining an excellent Web site, offering $2,000 Prairie Builder Internships to college students, and supporting refuge activities such as the Sow Your Wild Oats Festival, Buffalo Day, and "Ding" Darling Day.

The guiding principle behind the Neal Smith NWR is captured by a quote from Aldo Leopold: "The first law of intelligent tinkering is to save all the pieces." Judging by this measure, the restoration team at the refuge is full of intelligent tinkerers.

The Neal Smith Prairie Learning Center fits into the landscape.

Cypress and prairie at last light at
the Okefenokee NWR.

RIGHT: American alligator
floating at the surface of the
swamp's dark, still waters at the
Okefenokee NWR.

OKEFENOKEE

The Okefenokee NWR is mysterious, primeval, and beautiful. Located in the southeastern corner of Georgia and reaching a short way into Florida, the 396,000-acre refuge encompasses the vast majority of the 438,000-acre Okefenokee Swamp, one of the most famous freshwater wetlands in the world. The name of the swamp is a Europeanized version of a Choctaw Indian word, *owaquaphenoga,* which means "trembling earth." And there certainly is plenty of that. Throughout most of the swamp, sphagnum moss and other bog plants have, through their life and death over thousands of years, created a peat layer, 15 feet deep in places, that soaks up water like a thirsty sponge. Viewed from afar, the peat layer appears firm, but underfoot it will quake, causing nearby shrubs, bushes, and trees to shake slightly.

Less than 5 percent of the Okefenokee NWR, which the locals call "our swamp," is solid land. The rest is made up of floating and stationary peat islands and expanses of open water called "prairies." The origin of the swamp goes back 250,000 years. The retreating Atlantic Ocean left behind a saucer-shaped depression. As this remnant of the ocean floor filled with countless generations of plants and sediment, it rose up to the point that the swamp now sits between 103 to 128 feet above sea level and higher than the surrounding coastal plain. The swamp, therefore, is an exporter of water, serving as the headwaters for two rivers, the Suwannee, which drains southwest to the Gulf of Mexico, and the St. Mary's, which forms the boundary between Georgia and Florida and outlets to the Atlantic. The tannic acids released by decaying vegetation have turned the slow-moving waters of the Okefenokee NWR tea colored and made them as acidic as cola.

Each year, more than four hundred thousand people experience the Okefenokee NWR. Hiking on trails or canoeing through the swamp, visitors can see an impressive array of plant and animal life. On the peat hammocks, or "houses," carnivorous pitcher plants and bladderworts, along with ferns, grow next to towering cypress trees, a few more than five hundred years old, that have branches draped with flowing strands of Spanish moss. In silhouette the moss-cloaked trees look like ghostly sentinels, and one could imagine them guarding the secrets of the swamp. On the land, canebreak rattlesnakes, gopher tortoises, gray foxes, and wild turkeys make their way, seeking food and shelter. Some visitors will catch a glimpse of one of the four hundred black bears that wander the swamp. The Okefenokee

White ibis at the Okefenokee NWR.

RIGHT: Canoe trail through cypress at the Okefenokee NWR.

NWR's avian complement includes white ibises, pied-billed grebes, ring-necked ducks, whippoor-wills, anhingas, loggerhead shrikes, red-shouldered hawks, and endangered red-cockaded woodpeckers and wood storks. On the dark, smooth, and glasslike water, rafts of lilies and "neverwets" give purchase to tiny Florida cricket frogs and provide shade for passing Okefenokee pygmy sunfishes or chain pickerels. And then there are the alligators, a species that is nearly synonymous with the swamp.

The human history of the Okefenokee extends back to the Deptford, Swift Creek, and Weeden cultures that lived in the swamp as early as 2,500 years ago. Around 1500, Seminole Indians came to the area. In the 1830s Seminole raids on the local inhabitants raised the ire of the U.S. government, and Georgia-born General Charles Floyd was sent in on November 11, 1838, to remove the Seminoles to the West. Floyd and his 250 men routed the Seminoles, who were reportedly led by Holato

Micco, better known as Billy Bowlegs. But instead of moving west, the Seminoles went south and resettled in southern Florida.

The next attack on Okefenokee was mercan-tile, not military. In the late 1800s Captain Henry Jackson, a prominent Atlanta lawyer, spearheaded an effort to drain the swamp to make way for farming and timbering operations. The state of Georgia granted the lands to Jackson's Suwannee Canal Company, and soon men and machines went to work. Digging the canal, however, was no easy task. Swarming and ravenous mosquitoes, yellow flies, and ticks tormented the perpetually soaked workers. They had to contend with thick, oozing mud, falling trees, rolling logs, and water-logged canal walls that often caved in on them-selves soon after being dug. After five years of backbreaking work and millions of dollars spent, the canal was only 11.5 miles long. The Suwannee Canal Company, facing a national recession and

many years from even the possibility of turning a profit, gave up. Visitors to the Okefenokee NWR can still walk or boat along Canal Diggers Trail and see the scars in the landscape created by "Jackson's Folly."

In 1899 the Suwannee Canal Company sold its Okefenokee holdings to the Hebard Cypress Company of Philadelphia, which hungrily eyed the swamp's stands of old-growth cypress. What was needed was a means of getting the wood out

quickly and economically. To do this, Hebard drove pilings through the unstable peat layer deep into the firm sand below, and a rail line was then built atop the pilings to haul cut trees to a local sawmill. By 1927, when most logging operations ceased, 431 million board feet were removed. In 1937 the swamp was made a refuge when the federal government purchased it for $1.50 an acre. At the time Ira Gabrielson, head of the Bureau of Biological Survey, stated that the "establishment of the Okefenokee Refuge insures the preservation for posterity of one of the most interesting natural features in our country. Among the fresh-water swamps east of the Mississippi River it is exceeded only in size by the Everglades, and its variety and richness in animal and plant life have few, if any, counterparts."

Since its creation the Okefenokee NWR has benefited immensely from the work of CCC boys, refuge staff, and volunteers, whose time and effort have helped with the process of restoring the swamp to its original splendor. Protecting the Okefenokee NWR was given an added boost in 1974 when 353,000 acres of the refuge were designated as wilderness, making it the third largest wilderness area in the eastern United States. Visitors who want to venture into the heart of the swamp can sign up for one of the seven overnight shelters in the refuge. But they are forewarned that it is a true wilderness experience. The permit system ensures that each party spends each day and night alone, with only the swamp and its animal inhabitants for company.

Each year during National Wildlife Refuge Week the refuge celebrates Swamp Heritage Day. This includes a parade in nearby Folkston and numerous activities at the refuge's Chesser Island, a place that the Chesser family settled in the late 1880s and where some of the family stayed on until 1958. At the Chesser Island homestead, visitors get to enjoy homemade food cooked on a woodstove, listen to bluegrass music, and watch demonstrations of quilting, blacksmithing, basket weaving, and soap making. The day is capped off with a street dance in Folkston.

Despite its status as a refuge and a wilderness area, the Okefenokee NWR still faces threats from development. In the mid-1990s DuPont Company announced plans to build a titanium mine on the 38,000 acres of the Okefenokee Swamp it owns along the eastern border of the refuge. As the outlines of the proposed mine became clear, local, state, and federal opposition developed. Concerns centered on the potential for habitat loss for endangered species, wetland destruction, hydrologic alterations, and noise, water, air, and light pollution. At the time then–Secretary of the Interior Bruce Babbitt said that the mine "is not an appropriate neighbor for a national wildlife refuge." In 1999, after an 18-month facilitated negotiation process, a group that included DuPont, landowners, environmental groups, local and county governments, and others reached an agreement on a pact that held out the possibility of eliminating mining in the area. Central to the agreement was the idea that public and private funds could be raised to purchase the mineral rights from DuPont, in effect paying it not to mine. The price tag was $90 million. Some viewed the cost as too high. Babbitt stated that he had "strong reservations about the buyout," calling the cost "grossly inflated." As these words are being penned, despite active lobbying in Congress and efforts to garner private support, no funds have been raised. It is not clear how much longer DuPont will put off its plans to mine on the chance that funds will become available.

PETIT MANAN

Counting terns can be hazardous to one's health and wardrobe. The problem is adult terns don't much like having human researchers traipse over their nesting grounds counting eggs, no matter how well intentioned those humans might be. And to show their displeasure, the birds will dive-bomb the interlopers, sometimes drawing blood. Fortunately for the researchers, terns tend to aim for the highest point on the victim, making a stick taped to the back of a researcher's head a must—an avian lightning rod of sorts. But the stick won't deflect the inevitable white-

Cobbled coastline at low tide at the Petit Manan NWR.

RIGHT: Common terns feeding chick at the Petit Manan NWR.

wash falling from the sky. The researcher's only hope then is that the birds can't aim. Still, despite the potential discomfort, refuge staff eagerly look forward to the annual tern census on Petit Manan Island, which is part of the 7,300-acre Petit Manan NWR Complex. After all, it's exciting to participate in the very successful tern restoration project in the Gulf of Maine.

The Petit Manan NWR Complex includes five refuges along the coast of Maine. All told, the complex stretches for 200 miles, with forty-two islands and three shoreside parcels. All of the refuges have as their primary goal the restoration of colonial seabirds, such as common, Arctic, and endangered roseate terns, as well as Atlantic puffins, razorbills, black guillemots,

Leach's storm petrels, laughing gulls, and common eiders. The refuges also share the same tragic history that necessitated a restoration program in the first place.

Hundreds of years ago, Maine's coastal islands were home to large and healthy populations of colonial seabirds, and for good reasons. The islands were treeless, a key requirement for seabird habitat. Separation from the mainland afforded protection from land-based predators who either couldn't or wouldn't take a swim for a meal. Even winged predators such as the great horned owl might be dissuaded from dining out on an island if it were too far from their home base. And the cool, deep, turbulent waters surrounding the islands provided plentiful fish that the seabirds could eat and feed to their young.

Although Native Americans had inhabited some of the coastal islands for thousands of years, not until the settlement of the Europeans beginning in the 1600s did the birds began to feel real pressure from humans. Over the next few centuries, as farming and the raising of hogs and pigs spread to many of the islands, birds were forced out of their historical nesting sites. And during the latter part of the 1800s, numerous seabirds

mon and Arctic tern populations reached almost sixteen thousand pairs, a solid increase from earlier years. But then other ills visited the terns. The spread of open landfills and increases in fishery waste acted as magnets to herring and great black-backed gulls. These aggressive birds wreaked havoc on tern populations. Gulls nest earlier than terns and, therefore, managed to claim many of the best spots. Gulls also preyed on tern eggs and chicks. By 1977 the number of tern pairs in the

were killed for their plumage to satisfy women's fashions, and many eggs were taken to eat or for scientific purposes. As a result, by the turn of the twentieth century, colonial seabird populations in Maine were in dire straits.

About that time, however, pressures on the birds eased. Decreased reliance on boats as a form of travel and increased shoreside development led many islanders to relocate inland. Bird populations rebounded, especially terns. In 1940 com-

region had plummeted to five thousand. The Petit Manan NWR (in 1974) and other refuges in the complex were established to turn the tide.

To help the birds rebound, the Fish and Wildlife Service joined forces with a team of public and private organizations to form the Gulf of Maine Seabird Working Group, which includes the Maine Department of Inland Fisheries and Wildlife, the College of the Atlantic, the National Audubon Society, the Maine Audubon Society,

and the Canadian Wildlife Service. The Fish and
Wildlife Service and its partners employ a variety
of techniques in their tern restoration work. First,
the islands have to be made suitable for recolo-
nization. This means getting rid of the birds' main
competitors, the gulls. The mere presence of
humans at the outset of the nesting season is
often enough to achieve this goal. If that doesn't
work, a hierarchy of steps is employed, from making noise and destroying eggs and nests to limited
shooting and the use of avicides. The eviction of
the gulls sometimes is enough to lure the terns
back. Where the islands have not had tern borders
for many years, a bit more enticement is necessary, including using recordings of tern-colony
noises and tern decoys. The tern restoration began
in 1984 on two islands in the refuge complex,
Petit Manan and Seal, both of which currently
host healthy populations of common, Arctic, and
roseate terns, as well as a range of other seabirds.
Five other islands in the Petit Manan NWR
Complex have successful restoration projects, and
the plan is to expand the restoration efforts to
additional islands.

The Petit Manan NWR Complex is not only
for the colonial nesting seabirds. The complex
serves as a "bed and breakfast" for shorebirds,
songbirds, and waterfowl, as well as bald eagles
and wading birds that inhabit the complex's
wooded islands. On the 2,166-acre Petit Manan
Point, one can find a range of nonbird species,
including white-tailed deer, snowshoe hares, por-
cupines, coyotes, and ruffed and spruce grouse.

Eight islands in the Petit Manan NWR
Complex boast historic lighthouses, reminders of
the grave dangers mariners face off of Maine's
rocky and windswept coast. The one on Petit
Manan is located 14 miles off the mainland from
Bar Harbor, a particularly good place for a lighthouse. President James Monroe authorized construction of the lighthouse in 1817 in order to
help seafarers better negotiate the dangerous
sandbar that ran between the point and the
island. Such help was especially needed because
this area is one of the foggiest stretches of the
notoriously foggy Maine coast. The original
lighthouse was rebuilt in 1855 with Maine granite
and currently towers 123 feet above mean high
water, making it the second tallest lighthouse in
the state. According to the 1886 book *All Among
the Lighthouses or the Cruise of the Goldenrod* by
Mary Bradford Crowninshield, the Petit Manan
lighthouse was a real hazard for birds. The book
tells of an inspector finding the ground outside
of the lighthouse littered with avian casualties.
Commenting on the scene, the keeper said,
"They often fly against the lantern. Many a
time, in a high wind, I hear 'em flappin' against
the glass, an' I wonder if they don't obscure the
light when they come in such numbers."

Visitors to Petit Manan Point can stroll along
one of the refuge trails, passing jack pine stands,
blueberry barrens, cedar swamps, cobbled
beaches, coastal raised peatlands, and saltwater
marshes with green, spiky spartina grasses shifting
in the wind. The 1.5-mile Hollingsworth Trail is
named after John Hollingsworth, one of the photographers for this book. Given how much time
and effort he gave to documenting the refuge
system, this honor is especially appropriate.

CONCLUSION

In its first hundred years the refuge system accomplished great things. It set aside 95 million acres of precious wildlife habitat, protecting significant numbers of species of animals, plants, and insects, and in the process ensured that this country's critically important connection to nature remained vital and strong. The first hundred years were also a time when a lack of direction, money, and staffing kept the refuge system from fulfilling its full potential.

As the refuge system heads into its second century, its future looks bright. With an organic act in place, the goals of the refuge system are clear—wildlife comes first and other uses are allowed only when the well-being of wildlife will not be compromised. Recent budget increases, if built upon in the future, hold out the prospect of someday paring away and, hopefully, eliminating the massive backlog of operational and maintenance needs that are weighing down the refuge system.

Cypress and reflections in Monopoly Marsh at the Mingo NWR, Missouri.

And the centennial celebrations will energize the process of introducing and reintroducing Americans to their refuge system.

Tree snail on prickly pear cactus at the Santa Ana NWR, Texas.

RIGHT: Eastern gray wolf at the Agassiz NWR, Minnesota.

Steering the refuge system over the next hundred years will not be easy. Managing wildlife is hard work, made more difficult by the complex makeup of the refuge system and its many, at times competing, constituencies. Public and economic uses of refuges must be carefully designed and implemented to ensure that they are compatible with the purposes for which the refuges were established. The spread of development and the corresponding decrease in the country's reserves of wild and open spaces will place added pressures on the refuge system as people, weary of manufactured landscapes, seek out the pleasures that nature provides. While the refuge system should welcome more visitors, it must guard against the dangers of being loved too much. Also, as the refuge system adds more units, its need for funding will grow. Thus, even if efforts to fully fund existing operational and maintenance needs are successful, other financial battles will still need to be fought in the future.

The United States made an unparalleled commitment to protecting and preserving wildlife through the creation and growth of a refuge system that is not only one of this country's greatest conservation success stories but also an important part of the American experience. Every day the refuge system enriches people's lives, and it could do the same for the generations yet to come.

BIBLIOGRAPHY

Listed here are the main publications used in writing this book. This bibliography is not a complete record of all the sources consulted. It contains the primary materials and is intended to serve as a guide for those who are interested in learning more about the refuge system. A few sources deserve special mention because they provided a great range of information and, for the most part, are not individually referenced below. First on this list is Bill Reffalt. He has collected an enormous number of documents on the refuge system and has freely shared information as well as his time and personal knowledge with the author of this book. Bill's series of articles on the origins of the refuge system, which are mostly in press and will be published in future issues of *Fish and Wildlife News,* proved particularly helpful. Another individual who deserves special recognition is Jim Clark. His quarterly publication, the *Refuge Reporter,* which during its first few years he produced with his late wife, Mildred, is devoted exclusively to news and commentary on the refuge system. At the outset of this project, Jim sent the author a complete set of the *Refuge Reporter,* going back to 1992, and its contents have been an invaluable source of background information (those interested in learning more about this publication, can contact Jim at Avocet Crossing, Millwood, Virginia

22646–0156). The author also benefited from being able to review copies of *The Blue Goose Flyer,* the National Wildlife Refuge Association's quarterly newsletter (to learn more about this publication and the association, write to the NWRA at 1010 Wisconsin Ave. NW, Suite 200, Washington, D.C. 20007).

Also, the mere listing of George Laycock's two books on the refuge system does not do justice to their value to this endeavor. His books, particularly the stories of the Darling-Salyer years at the Bureau of Biological Survey in the 1930s and others from the early 1950s, were invaluable to the author of this book. In many instances Laycock's books provided unique source material for key events. The author's greatest debt, however, is to the U.S. Fish and Wildlife Service. For more than a century, the service and its predecessors have published a huge volume of press releases, policies, pamphlets, reports, bulletins, Web sites, and other documents pertaining to the refuge system that the author used extensively, only a few of which are listed below. Similarly, the author benefited greatly from interviews and discussions with Fish and Wildlife Service employees and individuals from other organizations that have a stake in the refuge system, and those individuals are thanked in the acknowledgments.

CHAPTER 2

Allen, Durward L. *Our Wildlife Legacy.* New York: Funk and Wagnalls Company, 1962.

Cameron, Jenks. *The Bureau of Biological Survey: Its History, Activities, and Organization.* Baltimore: Johns Hopkins Press, 1929.

Cronon, William. *Changes in the Land: Indians, Colonists, and the Ecology of New England.* New York: Hill and Wang, 1983.

Cutright, Paul Russell. *Theodore Roosevelt the Naturalist.* New York: Harper and Brothers, 1956.

Dolin, Eric Jay. *The U.S. Fish and Wildlife Service.* New York: Chelsea House Publishers, 1989.

Dolin, Eric Jay and Bob Dumaine. *The Duck Stamp Story: Art-Conservation-History.* Iola, Wisconsin: Krause Publications, 2001.

Geist, Valerius. *Buffalo Nation.* Stillwater, Minnesota: Voyageur Press, 1996.

Gilmore, Jene C. *Art for Conservation: The Federal Duck Stamp.* Barre, Massachusetts: Barre Publishers, 1971.

Grove, Noel. *Wild Lands for Wildlife: America's National Refuges.* Washington, D.C.: National Geographic Society, 1984.

Hogner, Dorothy Childs. *Conservation in America.* Philadelphia and New York: J. B. Lippincott Company, 1958.

Mathiesson, Peter. *Wildlife in America.* New York: Elisabeth Sifton Books, Viking, 1987.

Mitchell, John G. "Behind the Waterfall." *Wilderness* 47, no. 162 (fall 1983): 411.

Morris, Edmund. *Theodore Rex.* New York: Random House, 2001.

Murphy, Robert. *Wild Sanctuaries: Our National Wildlife Refuges—A Heritage Restored.* New York: E. P. Dutton.

Palmer, T. S. *Chronology and Index of the More Important Events in American Game Protection, 1776–1911.* U.S. Department of Agriculture, Biological Survey, bulletin no. 41, 1911. Washington, D.C.: U.S. Government Printing Office, 1912.

Partello, J. M. "Extermination of the Bison: A Thrilling Story of an Encounter a Dozen Years Ago." *The New York Times,* July 29, 1894.

Price, Jennifer. *Flight Maps.* New York: Basic Books, 1999.

Reiger, George. *The Wings of Dawn: The Complete Book of North American Waterfowling.* New York: Stein and Day, 1980.

Roe, F. G. *The North American Buffalo.* Toronto: University of Toronto Press, 1970.

Trefethen, James B. *An American Crusade for Wildlife.* New York: Winchester Press and Boone and Crockett Club, 1975.

Udall, Stewart. *The Quiet Crisis.* New York: Avon Books, 1963.

CHAPTER 3

Allen, J. A. "The Present Wholesale Destruction of Bird-Life in the United States." *Science—Supplement* 8, no. 160 (February 26, 1886): 194.

American Ornithological Union. "Bird-Laws." *Science—Supplement* 8, no. 160 (February 26, 1886): 202–4.

Cleveland, Grover. *Fishing and Shooting Sketches.* New York: Outing Publishing Company, 1906.

Dolin, Eric Jay and Bob Dumaine. *The Duck Stamp Story: Art-Conservation-History.* Iola, Wisconsin: Krause Publications, 2001.

Fox, Stephen. *John Muir and His Legacy: The American Conservation Movement.* Boston: Little, Brown and Company, 1981.

Graham, Frank Jr. and Carl W. Buchheister. *The Audubon Ark: A History of the National Audubon Society.* Austin: University of Texas Press, 1990.

Harrison, Benjamin. Proclamation no. 39, by the president of the United States of America, December 24, 1892.

Mathiesson, Peter. *Wildlife in America.* New York: Elisabeth Sifton Books, Viking, 1987.

Murphy, Robert. *Wild Sanctuaries: Our National Wildlife Refuges—A Heritage Restored.* New York: E. P. Dutton.

Nash, Roderick Frazier. *The Rights of Nature: A History of Environmental Ethics.* Madison: University of Wisconsin Press, 1989.

Palmer, T. S. *Chronology and Index of the More Important Events in American Game Protection, 1776–1911.* U.S. Department of Agriculture, Biological Survey, bulletin no. 41. Washington, D.C.: U.S. Government Printing Office, 1912.

"The Reservation of Afognak." *Forest and Stream* XL, no. 2 (January 12, 1893): 1.

Sennett, George B. "Destruction of the Eggs of Birds for Food." *Science—Supplement,* February 26, 1886, pp. 199–201.

Thaxter, Celia. "Woman's Heartlessness." *Audubon Magazine,* February 1987, pp. 13–14.

Thoreau, Henry David. *Thoreau on Birds: Notes on New England Birds from the Journals of Henry David Thoreau.* Boston: Beacon Press, 1993.

Trefethen, James B. *An American Crusade for Wildlife.* New York: Winchester Press and Boone and Crockett Club, 1975.

Van Name, W. G. "Government Game Preserves for the Protection of Migratory Game Birds." *Forest and Stream,* June 5, 1897, p. 446.

Weed, Clarence M. and Ned Dearborn. *Birds in Their Relations to Man: A Manual of Economic Ornithology for the United States and Canada.* Philadelphia and London: J. B. Lippincott Company, 1903.

Wright, Mabel Osgood. "Keep on Pedaling!" *Bird-Lore,* February 1, 1901, pp. 33–34.

CHAPTER 4

Chadwick, Douglas. "National Wildlife Refuges." *National Geographic* 190, no. 4 (October 1996): 2–35.

Chapman, Frank M. "Pelican Island Revisited." *Bird-Lore,* January–February 1901, pp. 3–8.

Clark, Jim. "Cypress Creek National Wildlife Refuge." *Refuge Reporter* 7, no. 2 (summer 1999): 5–8.

Cox, Elbert, regional director of the southeast region, National Park Service. Speech given at the dedication of Pelican Island as a Registered National Historic Landmark, November 14, 1963.

Day, Albert M. *North American Waterfowl.* New York: Stackpole and Heck, 1949.

Dutcher, William. "The Millinery Trade Organ." *Bird-Lore,* March–April 1906, p. 72.

———. "Reservation News." *Bird-Lore,* July–August 1906, p. 145.

———. "Annual Report of the National Association of Audubon Societies for 1906." *Bird-Lore,* November–December 1906, pp. 224–47.

F. M. C. "A Remarkable Bonnet." *Bird-Lore,* October 1900, p. 166.

Graham, Frank Jr. *Man's Dominion: The Story of Conservation in America.* New York: M. Evans and Company, 1971.

Graham, Frank Jr. and Carl W. Buchheister. *The Audubon Ark: A History of the National Audubon Society.* Austin: University of Texas Press, 1990.

Henshall, James A. *Camping and Cruising in Florida: An Account of Two Winters Passed in Cruising around the Coasts of Florida.* Cincinnati: Robert Clark and Company, 1884.

Laycock, George. *The Sign of the Flying Goose: A Guide to the National Wildlife Refuges.* New York: Natural History Press, 1965.

Reffalt, William C. *Historical Chronology: The National Wildlife Refuge System*. Report presented at the Refuge Management Training Academy in Charleston, South Carolina, February 2, 1994.

————. "A Prologue to Pelican Island." *Fish and Wildlife News,* October/November/December 2001, p. 31.

U.S. Fish and Wildlife Service. "Refuge System Celebrates Anniversary: 75 Years and Going Strong." *Fish and Wildlife News, Special Edition,* December 1978–January 1979. Washington, D.C.: U.S. Government Printing Office.

"Wholesale Destruction of Birds in Florida." *Audubon Magazine,* September 1887, pp. 178–80.

Wright, Mabel Osgood. "Back to First Principles." *Bird-Lore,* September–October 1902, pp. 168–71.

CHAPTER 5

Audubon Department. *Bird-Lore,* July–August 1906, 145.

Cameron, Jenks. *The Bureau of Biological Survey: Its History, Activities, and Organization.* Baltimore: Johns Hopkins Press, 1929.

Cutright, Paul Russell. *Theodore Roosevelt the Naturalist.* New York: Harper and Brothers, 1956.

Dutcher, William. "Some Reasons Why International Bird Protection Is Necessary." *Bird-Lore,* May–June 1910, pp. 169–72.

Fox, Stephen. *John Muir and His Legacy: The American Conservation Movement.* Boston: Little, Brown and Company, 1981.

Henshaw, Henry W. "Our Mid-Pacific Bird Reservation." In *Yearbook of the Department of Agriculture.* Washington, D.C.: U.S. Government Printing Office, 1911.

Laycock, George. *Wild Refuge.* New York: Natural History Press, 1969. 103.

Morris, Edmund. *Theodore Rex.* New York: Random House, 2001.

Roosevelt, Theodore. *Theodore Roosevelt, an Autobiography.* New York: Macmillan Company, 1913.

————. *A Book-Lover's Holidays in the Open.* New York: Charles Scribner's Sons, 1916.

Trefethen, James B. *An American Crusade for Wildlife.* New York: Winchester Press and Boone and Crockett Club, 1975.

U.S. House of Representatives, Committee on the Public Lands. *Loch-Katrine Bird Reservation: Correspondence between Hon. F.* W. Mondell and Dr. T. S. Palmer relative to Executive Authority for the Reservation of Lands as Bird Preserves. Washington, D.C.: U.S. Government Printing Office, 1909.

————. *Congressional Record.* February 11, 1909, p. 2215.

CHAPTER 6

Dolin, Eric Jay and Bob Dumaine. *The Duck Stamp Story: Art-Conservation-History.* Iola, Wisconsin: Krause Publications, 2001.

Fox, Stephen. *John Muir and His Legacy: The American Conservation Movement.* Boston: Little, Brown and Company, 1981.

Gabrielson, Ira N. *Wildlife Refuges.* New York: Macmillan Company, 1943.

Laycock, George. *The Sign of the Flying Goose: A Guide to the National Wildlife Refuges.* New York: Natural History Press, 1965.

Trefethen, James B. *An American Crusade for Wildlife.* New York: Winchester Press and Boone and Crockett Club, 1975.

Wilson, Vanez T. and Rachel L. Carson. "Bear River: A National Wildlife Refuge." *Conservation in Action, Number Eight.* Washington D.C.: U.S. Fish and Wildlife Service, U.S. Government Printing Office, 1950.

CHAPTER 7

Dolin, Eric Jay and Bob Dumaine. *The Duck Stamp Story: Art-Conservation-History.* Iola, Wisconsin: Krause Publications, 2001.

Holland, Linda. "A Golden Anniversary." *Field and Stream,* March 1984.

Holland, Ray P. "Bulletin of the American Game Protective Association." *Field and Stream,* July 1920.

————. "A Law at Last!" *Field and Stream,* May 1934, 28–29, 66.

Palmer, T. S. "Some Fundamental Principles of Bird Laws." *Bird-Lore,* April 1901, pp. 79–81.

Shiras, George III. "Federal Protection of Wildfowl." *Forest and Stream,* supplement (November 24, 1906): 815–24.

Trefethen, James B. *An American Crusade for Wildlife.* New York: Winchester Press and Boone and Crockett Club, 1975.

CHAPTER 8

Clark, James. "Hart Mountain National Antelope Refuge." *Refuge Reporter* 4, no. 3 (spring 1996): 10–13.

Darling, Jay N. "The Story of the Wildlife Refuge System: Part I." *National Parks Magazine,* January–March 1954, pp. 6–10, 43–46.

————. "The Story of the Wildlife Refuge Program: Part II." *National Parks Magazine,* April–June 1954, pp. 53–56, 86–91.

Dolin, Eric Jay. "Bucks for Ducks." *American Philatelist* 111, no. 8 (August 1997): 728–40.

Dolin, Eric Jay and Bob Dumaine. *The Duck Stamp Story: Art-Conservation-History.* Iola, Wisconsin: Krause Publications, 2001.

Hawkins, A. S., R. C. Hansen, H. K. Nelson, and H. M. Reeves. *Flyways: Pioneering Waterfowl Management in North America.* Washington, D.C.: U.S. Department of Interior and the Fish and Wildlife Service, 1984.

Johnson, Laurence F. *Federal Duck Stamp Story: Fifty Years of Excellence.* Davenport, Iowa: Alexander and Company, 1984.

Laycock, George. *The Sign of the Flying Goose: A Guide to the National Wildlife Refuges.* New York: Natural History Press, 1965.

Lendt, David L. *Ding: The Life of Jay Norwood Darling.* Ames: Iowa State University Press, 1979.

Manning, Phillip. *Islands of Hope.* Winston-Salem, North Carolina: John F. Blair, 1999.

McBride, David P. *The Federal Duck Stamps.* Piscataway, New Jersey: Winchester Press, 1984.

Shoemaker, Carl D. *The Stories behind the Organization of the National Wildlife Federation and Its Early Struggles for Survival.* Washington, D.C.: Carl D. Shoemaker, 1960.

Worster, Donald. *Dust Bowl: The Southern Plains in the 1930s.* New York: Oxford University Press, 1979.

CHAPTER 9

Bailey, James A., William Elder, and Ted D. McKinney, eds. *Readings in Wildlife Conservation.* Washington, D.C.: Wildlife Society, 1974.

Butcher, Devereux. *Seeing America's Wildlife.* New York: Devin-Adair Company, 1955.

Carson, Rachel L. "Chincoteague: A National Wildlife Refuge." *Conservation in Action, Number One.* Washington D.C.: U.S. Fish and Wildlife Service, U.S. Government Printing Office, 1947.

————. "Parker River National Wildlife Refuge." *Conservation in Action, Number Two.* Washington D.C.: U.S. Fish and Wildlife Service, U.S. Government Printing Office, 1947.

————. "Mattamuskeet: A National Wildlife Refuge." *Conservation in Action, Number*

Four. Washington D.C.: U.S. Fish and Wildlife Service, U.S. Government Printing Office, 1947.

———. "Guarding Our Wildlife Resources." *Conservation in Action, Number Five.* Washington, D.C.: U.S. Fish and Wildlife Service, U.S. Government Printing Office, 1948.

Clark, James. "Research Is Our Mission: Patuxent—One of a Kind Refuge Has Unique 60-Year History." *Refuge Reporter* 4, no. 2 (winter 1995): 6–9.

———. "Rice Lake National Wildlife Refuge." *Refuge Reporter* 5, no. 4 (summer 1997): 9–11.

———. "Horicon National Wildlife Refuge." *Refuge Reporter* 6, no. 4 (summer 1998): 5–7.

Darling, Jay N. "The Story of the Wildlife Refuge Program: Part II." *National Parks Magazine,* April–June 1954, pp. 53–56, 86–91.

Laycock, George. *The Sign of the Flying Goose: A Guide to the National Wildlife Refuges.* New York: Natural History Press, 1965.

Lear, Linda. *Rachel Carson: Witness for Nature.* New York: Henry Holt and Company, 1997.

Lendt, David L. *Ding: The Life of Jay Norwood Darling.* Ames: Iowa State University Press, 1979.

Linduska, Joseph P., ed. *Waterfowl Tomorrow.* Washington, D.C.: U.S. Fish and Wildlife Service, U.S. Government Printing Office, 1964.

Mathiesson, Peter. *Wildlife in America.* New York: Elisabeth Sifton Books, Viking, 1987.

Nash, Roderick Frazier, ed. *American Environmentalism: Readings in Conservation History.* New York: McGraw-Hill Publishing Company, 1990.

Stroud, Richard H., ed. *National Leaders of American Conservation.* Washington, D.C.: Smithsonian Institution Press, 1985.

Trefethen, James B. *An American Crusade for Wildlife.* New York: Winchester Press and Boone and Crockett Club, 1975.

Wilson, Vanez T. and Rachel L. Carson. "Bear River: A National Wildlife Refuge." *Conservation in Action, Number Eight.* Washington D.C.: U.S. Fish and Wildlife Service, U.S. Government Printing Office, 1950.

CHAPTER 10

Chandler, William J. "The U.S. Fish and Wildlife Service." In *The Audubon Wildlife Report, 1985,* edited by Amos S. Eno and Roger L. DiSilvestro. New York: National Audubon Society, 1985.

Clark, Jim. "Waterfowl Production Areas: Prairie Jewels of the Refuge System." *Refuge Reporter* 7, no. 3 (spring 1999): 9–11.

Cottam, Clarence. "Report of Encroachments on National Wildlife Refuges." U.S. Fish and Wildlife Service, October 6, 1952 (internal memo).

Doherty, Jim. "Refuges on the Rocks." *Audubon,* July 1983, pp. 74–117.

Laycock, George. *The Sign of the Flying Goose: A Guide to the National Wildlife Refuges.* New York: Natural History Press, 1965.

Stoddart, Alexander. "Fishing and Hunting Presidents." *Forest and Stream,* January 1923, 8–10, 28.

Trefethen, James B. *An American Crusade for Wildlife.* New York: Winchester Press and Boone and Crockett Club, 1975.

Udall, Stewart. *The Quiet Crisis.* New York: Avon Books, 1963.

Williamson, Lonnie. "50 Years of Duck Stamps." *Outdoor Life,* July 1984, pp. 53, 62–66.

CHAPTER 11

Bean, Michael J. *The Evolution of National Wildlife Law.* New York: Praeger, 1983.

Clark, James. "Mason Neck NWR." *Refuge Reporter,* fall 1995, pp. 5–8.

———. "Crystal River National Wildlife Refuge." *Refuge Reporter* 6, no. 2 (winter 1997): 7–9.

———. "Alligator River National Wildlife Refuge." *Refuge Reporter* 10, no.1 (fall 2001): 5–8.

———. "Long Island National Wildlife Refuges." *Refuge Reporter* 10, no. 3 (spring 2002): 5–12.

DiSilvestro, Roger L., William J. Chandler, Katherine Barton, and Lillian Labate, eds. *Audubon Wildlife Report, 1987.* New York: National Audubon Society, 1986.

Eno, Amos, Roger L. DiSilvestro, and William J. Chandler, eds. *Audubon Wildlife Report, 1986.* New York: National Audubon Society, 1986.

International Crane Foundation Web site: www.savingcranes.org/species/whooping.asp.

Jackson, Gerry. "The ESA at Twenty-Five." *Endangered Species Bulletin,* U.S. Fish and Wildlife Service, 24, no. 1 (January/February 1999): 25.

Mantell, Michael, Phyllis Myers, and Robert B. Reed. "The Land and Water Conservation Fund: Past Experience, Future Directions." In *Audubon Wildlife Report, 1988–1989,* edited by

William J. Chandler and Lillian Labate, pp. 257–81. San Diego: Academic Press, 1988.

Mathiesson, Peter. *The Birds of Heaven: Travels with Cranes.* New York: North Point Press, 2001.

Operation Migration Web site: www.operationmigration.org.

Reffalt, Bill. *A Vision for Wilderness in the National Wildlife Refuge System.* Wilderness Resource Distinguished Lectureship 13. University of Idaho, Wilderness Research Center, March 3, 1994.

Whooping Crane Eastern Partnership Web site: www.bringbackthecranes.org.

Wilderness Society Web site: www.wilderness.org/standbylands/ wilderness/wildletter2.htm.

CHAPTER 12

Clark, Jim. "Montezuma: National Wildlife Refuge in New York State Is Named for Aztec Emperor." *Refuge Reporter* 5, no. 2 (winter 1996): 5–9.

Defenders of Wildlife. *A Report on the National Wildlife Refuge System.* Washington, D.C.: Defenders of Wildlife, 1977.

Doherty, Jim. "Refuges on the Rocks." *Audubon,* July 1983, pp. 74–117.

Fink, Richard J. "The National Wildlife Refuges: Theory, Practice and Prospect." *Harvard Environmental Law Review* 18, no. 1 (1994): 1–135.

Greenwalt, Lynn A. "The National Wildlife Refuge System." In *Wildlife in America,* edited by Howard P. Brokaw, pp. 399–412. Washington D.C.: Council on Environmental Quality, 1978.

Leopold, A. Starker, Clarence Cottam, Ian McT. Gowan, Ira N. Gabrielson, and Thomas L. Kimball. "The National Wildlife Refuge System: Report of the Advisory Committee on Wildlife Management, Appointed by Interior Secretary Stewart L. Udall." *Reports of the Special Advisory Board for the Secretary of the Interior, 1963–1968,* Thirty-third North American Wildlife Conference. Washington, D.C.: Wildlife Management Institute, 1969.

National Wildlife Refuge Study Task Force. *Recommendations on the Management of the National Wildlife Refuge System.* U.S. Fish and Wildlife Service, February 1978.

Reed, Nathaniel P. and Dennis Drabelle. *The United States Fish and Wildlife Service.* Boulder, Colorado: Westview Press, 1984.

U.S. Fish and Wildlife Service. *Final*

Recommendations on the Management of the National Wildlife Refuge System. Washington, D.C., April 1979.

CHAPTER 13

Corn, Lynne M., Bernard A. Gelb, and Pamela Baldwin. *The Arctic National Wildlife Refuge: The Next Chapter,* CRS Issue Brief for Congress. Washington, D.C.: Congressional Research Service, December 17, 2001.

Doherty, Jim. "Refuges on the Rocks." *Audubon,* July 1983, pp. 74–117.

Douglas, D.C., P. E. Reynolds, and E. B. Rhode, eds. *Arctic Refuge Coastal Plain Terrestrial Wildlife Research Summaries.* Washington, D.C.: U.S. Geological Survey, Biological Resources Division, Biological Sciences Report USGS/BRD/BSR-2002–0001.

Duscha, Julia. "Setting the Crown Jewels: How the Alaska Act Was Won." *Living Wilderness* 44, no. 152 (spring 1981): 4–17.

Florida PantherNet official education Web site: www.panther.state.fl.us/handbook/natural/whatname.html.

Foote, Timothy. "Where the Gooney Birds Are." *Smithsonian,* September 2001, pp. 89–97.

Grunwald, Michael. "Warnings on Drillings Reversed." *Washington Post,* April 7, 2002, pp. A1, A11.

Mitchell, John G. "Behind the Waterfall." *Wilderness* 47, no. 162 (fall 1983): 4–11.

Reffalt, William C. *Testimony before the Subcommittee on Environment and Natural Resources of the House Merchant Marine and Fisheries Regarding the National Wildlife Refuge System.* 103rd Congress, 2nd sess., August 9, 1994, serial no. 103–22; 74–85.

Ryden, Hope. "Conflict and Compatibility." *Wilderness* 47, no. 162 (fall 1983): 25–31.

U.S. Fish and Wildlife Service, Compatibility Task Force. *Report to the Director: A Review of Secondary Uses Occurring on National Wildlife Refuges,* June 1990.

U.S. General Accounting Office. *National Wildlife Refuges: Continuing Problems with Incompatible Uses Call for Bold Action.* Washington, D.C.: U.S. General Accounting Office, September 1989 (GAO/RCED-89 196).

———.*Wildlife Management: National Refuge Contamination Is Difficult to Confirm and Clean Up.* Washington, D.C.: U.S. General Accounting Office, July 1987 (GAO/RCED-87–128).

Wilderness Society. *Alaska National Interest Lands Conservation Act: Citizen's Guide.* Washington, D.C.: Wilderness Society, July 2001.

CHAPTER 14

Audubon Society. *America's Hidden Lands: A Proposal to Discover Our National Wildlife Refuge System,* 1999. On the Audubon Web site: www.audubon.org/campaign/refuge/actalert4.html.

———. *Refuges in Crisis,* 2001. On the Audubon Web site: www.audubon.org/campaign/refuge_report/index.html.

Cooperative Alliance for Refuge Enhancement. *Shortchanging America's Wildlife: A Report on the National Wildlife Refuge System Funding Crisis,* 2001. On the National Wildlife Refuge Association Web site: www.refugenet.org.

Defenders of Wildlife. *Putting Wildlife First: Recommendations for Reforming Our Troubled Refuge System.* Washington, D.C.: Defenders of Wildlife, March 1992.

Drabelle, Dennis. "Going It Alone: An Inside Look at a Vulnerable System." *Wilderness* 47, no. 162 (fall 1983): 12–24.

Laughland, Andrew and James Caudill. *Banking on Nature: The Economic Benefits to Local Communities of National Wildlife Refuge Visitation.* Washington, D.C.: U.S. Fish and Wildlife Service, July 1997.

Mitchell, John G. "Behind the Waterfall." *Wilderness* 47, no. 162 (fall 1983): 4–11.

National Wildlife Refuge Association. *Taking Flight: An Introduction to Building Refuge Friends Organizations,* 1997.

Neinaber, Jeanne Clark and Daniel C. McCool. *Staking out the Terrain: Power and Performance among Natural Resource Agencies,* second edition. Albany: State University of New York Press, 1996.

Reffalt, William C. "A Shelter for Refuges." *Wilderness,* summer 1987, p. 60.

U.S. Fish and Wildlife Service. *Fulfilling the Promise: The National Wildlife Refuge System,* July 1999.

CHAPTER 15

Audubon, John James. *Audubon, by Himself: A Profile of John James Audubon, from Writings Selected, Arranged and Edited by Alice Ford.* New York: Natural History Press, 1969.

Clark, James. "Okefenokee National Wildlife Refuge." *Refuge Reporter* 9, no. 3 (spring 2001): 5–10.

Crowninshield, Mary Bradford. *All among the Lighthouses or the Cruise of the Goldenrod.* Boston: D. Lothrop Company, 1886.

Hollingsworth, John and Karen Hollingsworth. *Seasons of the Wild.* Bellvue, Colorado: Worm Press, 1994.

Gibson, Daniel. *Audubon Guide to the National Wildlife Refuges: Southwest.* New York: Griffin Trade Paperback, 2000.

Gove, Doris. *Audubon Guide to the National Wildlife Refuges: Southeast.* New York: Griffin Trade Paperback, 2000.

Grassy, John. *Audubon Guide to the National Wildlife Refuges: Rocky Mountains.* New York: Griffin Trade Paperback, 2000.

Laubach, Rene. *Audubon Guide to the National Wildlife Refuges: New England.* New York: Griffin Trade Paperback, 2000.

MacArthur, Loren. *Audubon Guide to the National Wildlife Refuges: California and Hawaii.* New York: Griffin Trade Paperback, 2000.

MacArthur, Loren and Debbie S. Miller. *Audubon Guide to the National Wildlife Refuges: Alaska and the Northwest.* New York: Griffin Trade Paperback, 2000.

Margolin, Malcom. *The Ohlone Way: Indian Life in the San Francisco–Monterey Bay Area.* Berkley: Heyday Books, 1978.

Palmer, Bill. *Audubon Guide to the National Wildlife Refuges: South Central.* New York: Griffin Trade Paperback, 2000.

Powers, Tom and John Grassy. *Audubon Guide to the National Wildlife Refuges: Northern Midwest.* New York: Griffin Trade Paperback, 2000.

Public Broadcasting System Web site on Lewis and Clark, *The Journey of the Corps of Discovery:* www.pbs.org/lewisandclark.

Ricciuti, Edward R. *Audubon Guide to the National Wildlife Refuges: Mid-Atlantic.* New York: Griffin Trade Paperback, 2000.

Riley, Laura and William Riley. *Guide to the National Wildlife Refuges.* New York: Macmillan, 1992.

Russell, C. M. "Some Incidents of Western Life." *Scribner's Magazine* 37, no. 17 (February 1905): 158–63.

Wall, Dennis. *Western National Wildlife Refuges.* Santa Fe: Museum of New Mexico Press, 1996.

INDEX